CCM Certification
Made Easy

2nd Edition

Deanna Cooper Gillingham, RN, CCM

BLUE BAYOU PRESS

Credits

Content Editing: Anne Llewellyn, RN-BC, MS, BHSA, CCM, CRRN

Copy Editing: Andrea Morris

Cover Design: Judy Shriner

Published by Blue Bayou Press LLC
ISBN-13: 9781943889020
ISBN-10: 1943889023

DEDICATION

A huge thank you to Anne Llewellyn for all of her support, encouragement, suggestions, work, and advice during the writing of this book, as well as all the contributions she has made to the profession of case management. Anne currently is writing must read articles for case managers at nursesadvocates.net/

To Mom for showing me you can do anything you put your mind to and supporting all my crazy dreams.

To Abi for sharing my crazy dreams, and for doing everything else so I could write.

Contents

Care Delivery and Reimbursement Methods

Contents

Contents

Psychosocial Concepts and Support Systems   81

Contents

Quality and Outcomes Evaluations and Measurements 125

Contents

Rehabilitation Concepts and Strategies   157

Ethical, Legal and Practice Standards   175

Introduction

Congratulations on your decision to advance your career and obtain your Certified Case Manager (CCM) credential. Not long ago I was in your shoes, preparing to take the CCM Exam. I spent hundreds of hours reading books, in study groups, attending lectures, and searching the web. I was disappointed when I found many of the books available were written by test prep companies, not by case managers who have actually taken the exam. That may be why they did not address many of the items CCMC stated would be on the exam.

I was also frustrated when I found no information on some subjects and too many unnecessary details on others. I was looking for a concise resource without fluff, just facts. That is why I created this book. I took the information I found to help me pass the CCM and compiled it into an easy-to-read, fast-paced resource for you. The good news is you don't have to spend countless hours researching like I did. You have all the information you need right here!

How to use this book

The Commission for Case Manager Certification (CCMC) creates the CCM exam. According to their Exam Study Materials page, "The CCM exam is practice-based, meaning all questions are based around knowledge that an experienced case manager should know and understand. There isn't any course or education required to take the exam or to prepare for the exam."

The CCMC has provided us with a Glossary of Terms on their website. According to the CCMC, "The glossary of terms is a list of terms directly or indirectly related to the practice of case management compiled by members of CCMC's Exam and Research Committee...This list is not meant to be exhaustive...CCMC suggests that candidates for the CCM exam be familiar with terms and concepts relevant to case management.

This list should be helpful in that regard." For this reason, I have included a condensed version of the definitions from the CCMC's glossary of terms that are relevant to the chapters in this book. They can be found at the end of the book in the section titled "Glossary."

This book was created to provide fundamental information on each of the subject areas of the exam. At the end of each chapter I have provided links to additional information that you can review if you feel you need more information on a subject.

CCMC updates the exam approximately every five years, providing a new "exam blueprint" or outline with each update. This book has been organized according to the most recent outline provided by the CCMC. It may be read through from beginning to end, but that is not necessary. Because it may be read in sections, some information is repeated in more than one area when necessary.

Additional Resources

Every effort has been made to provide a firm foundation for the CCM Exam. However, I highly recommend reviewing the following:

The free resources available on the CCMC website when you apply for the exam.

The Case Management Society of America (CMSA) Standards of Practice for Case Management
http://solutions.cmsa.org/acton/media/10442/standards-of-practice-for-case-management

The Commission for Case Manager Certification glossary of terms
https://ccmcertification.org/sites/default/files/downloads/2011/CCMC%20
Glossary.pdf

The Commission for Case Manager Certification Professional Code of
Conduct
https://ccmcertification.org/sites/default/files/downloads/2012/Code%20
of%20Professional%20Conduct%20for%20Case%20Managers.pdf

Claim your free Companion Workbook

To receive your free PDF companion workbook to *CCM Cetification Made
Easy*, be sure to visit my website, Casemanagementstudyguide.com/pass/

While you're there, sign up for emails so you will be notified of additional
resources and information to help you pass the exam.

Chapter One:
Care Delivery and
Reimbursement Methods

A case manager must have broad knowledge of care delivery and reimbursement methods to perform her job effectively. She must understand the clinical and financial resources available to her client, as well as the eligibility criteria for receiving those resources. This will enable her to ensure the client receives the most appropriate care in a cost-effective manner.

Case Management Process and Tools

The Commission for Case Manager Certification (CCMC) defines case management as "a collaborative process that assesses, plans, implements, coordinates, monitors, and evaluates the options and services required to meet the client's health and human services needs. It is characterized by advocacy, communication, and resource management and promotes quality and cost-effective interventions and outcomes."

According to CCMC's Case Management Body of Knowledge, the case management process consists of:

- Screening
- Stratifying risk
- Assessing
- Planning
- Implementing (care coordination)
- Following-up
- Transitioning (transitional care)
- Communication post-transition
- Evaluation

These steps are not sequential, meaning case managers do not complete a phase and check it off their list as complete. Many phases will take place concurrently, or be revisited and repeated. For example, a new problem may arise during follow-up with a patient. The case manager would then return to the planning phase for that problem, while continuing to follow up on the original problem.

Screening

Case management is not for every client. During the screening phase, patient information is reviewed to decide the patient's appropriateness for case management services. Details obtained may include claims information, utilization of healthcare services, current health status, insurance eligibility, support system, and health history.

Depending on the program, clients may be appropriate for case management based on:

- Diagnosis
- High-dollar diagnosis
- High utilization (frequent hospital or emergency room visits)
- Poor pain control
- Chronic, catastrophic illness
- Social issues, such as a weak or nonexistent support system
- Difficult discharge planning
- Financial issues

Stratifying Risk

Case managers use biometric screening and health risk assessment tools to classify clients into low, moderate, or high risk categories. This allows for proper interventions based on the client's needs.

Risk stratification can also be done prior to screening to identify members who could benefit from case management. Many population management, chronic care management, and health insurance settings use technology to stratify risk and identify clients that may be most appropriate for their case management services. This technology may flag all cases with certain diagnoses, high-dollar claims, or frequent hospitalizations, for example.

Assessing

A comprehensive, needs-based assessment is conducted based on the case manager's practice setting to identify the client's problems, needs, and interests. The assessment can be done in person or telephonically. In addition to speaking with the client, information can also be obtained from family, caregivers, providers, medical records, insurance representatives, the client's employer, and other sources. This information is then used to create a case management plan of care. The assessment phase is similar to screening, but provides a more in-depth look into the client's healthcare situation. The assessment may include:

- Medical history
- Current medical conditions
- Functional status
- Cognitive status
- Health insurance status
- Spiritual life
- Psychosocial concerns
- Environment (e.g., living conditions)
- Vocational/educational status
- Financial status
- Support system
- Culture and language
- Self-care capability
- Health literacy
- Health goals
- Readiness to change
- Past and current service utilization
- Current medications
- Safety

Planning

The objective of this phase is to develop an individualized case management plan of care to address the identified needs. This should be done with input from the client and/or caregiver and other members of the healthcare team whenever possible. Short-term and long-term goals should be developed and prioritized, and interventions should be planned. The short-term goals should be directly related to the long-term goals. The interventions are the treatments, resources, and services needed to meet the client's needs and goals and should apply evidence-based standards and care guidelines. The acronym SMART is used to identify the attributes of effective goals.

- Specific
- Measurable
- Achievable
- Realistic
- Timely

The planning phase is completed after services, treatments, and resources needed are identified and authorizations are obtained from the payer.

Implementation

The case management plan is carried out during the implementation phase, also called care coordination. The interventions arranged in the planning phase are executed, coordinated, and secured. The case manager acts as a liaison between the client, caregivers, providers, and payer.

Following-Up/Monitoring

The case manager conducts ongoing assessments and gathers information from the patient, caregiver, and other relevant sources. This information is evaluated to determine the client's response to the current case management plan and the progress toward the desired outcomes. Modifications are made to the plan as needed, and ongoing follow-ups determine the effectiveness of the modifications.

Transitional Care

Transitions of care, whether across the health and human services continuum or to differing levels of care, put the client at increased risk for adverse events. (See section on Transitions of Care/Transitional Care.) Case managers provide a valuable service by overseeing the proper transition to the next level of care, as well as ensuring continuity of care.

During this phase the case manager prepares the client for discharge or transfer to another provider. He or she coordinates communication among the client, the current provider, the subsequent provider, and caregivers. The case manager also secures durable medical equipment and transportation when necessary.

Post-transition Communication

After a client transitions from an episode of care, the case manager contacts the client and/or caregiver to confirm a smooth transition. The case manager ensures post-transition services are being obtained, reconciles medications, and assesses for issues.

Evaluating Outcomes

The case manager assesses the effectiveness of the case management plan of care and its effect on the client's condition, and creates any associated reports.

The evaluation may focus on multiple aspects of care, including:

- A financial evaluation with a cost-benefit analysis and return on investment
- Clinical outcomes
- Quality of life
- Client satisfaction
- Self-care management ability
- Knowledge of health conditions and plan of care

Roles and Functions of Case Managers in Various Settings

Many case management roles and functions are the same regardless of setting, such as advocacy, assessment, planning, empowerment, facilitation, collaboration, and education. For example, all case managers conduct comprehensive assessments of the client's needs. From the assessment, the case manager develops a case management plan in collaboration with the patient and family.

Case managers also collaborate with the client and his or her family, caregiver, physician, provider, payer, and community to achieve quality, cost-efficient outcomes. This requires the case manager to facilitate communication and coordination between all members involved in the patient's care. He or she must also educate the client, family, and members of the healthcare team regarding treatment options, insurance benefits, and community resources to facilitate informed decision-making. This empowers the client and promotes self-advocacy.

Advocacy for both the client and the payer is another role of the case manager. The goal is to achieve the best outcome for the client, provider, and payer. If a conflict arises, the client's needs take priority.

The setting the case manager works in often determines the extent to which each of these functions is carried out. Further, unique roles and functions may exist in a particular case management setting. Below is a list of settings in which case managers practice, followed by functions of case managers in those settings.

1. Physician's offices, ambulatory care clinics, accountable care organizations, corporations, and community-based organizations, including healthcare centers and university clinics
   These roles are geared toward prevention.

   • Wellness programs

   • Screenings

   • Health risk assessments

- Risk-reduction strategies
- Telephonic triage
- Disease management
- Facilitating access to services
- Referrals to community-based resources
- Coordination of medical and social services
- Ensuring patient knowledge and compliance with treatment
- Monitoring

2. Hospitals
   - Utilization review
   - Discharge planning
   - Resource management
   - Coordination of care among team members
   - Transition to post-acute care

3. Acute inpatient rehabilitation, subacute care, long term acute care hospitals (LTAC), and skilled nursing facilities (SNF)
   - Coordinate interdisciplinary team (IDT) meetings
   - Verify benefits and authorization of services
   - Facilitate referrals
   - Discharge planning

4. Payer-based settings, including public health insurance programs (Medicare, Medicaid, state-funded programs) and private health insurance programs (occupational health, disability, group health insurance, managed care organizations)
   - Liaise between providers, members, and insurance company
   - Coordinate care
   - Ensure appropriate care

- Negotiate for services
- Monitor for compliance with treatment plan
- Ensure appropriate level of care and care setting
- Educate on healthcare benefits
- Utilization management
- Discharge planning

5. Palliative care, home care, and hospice care
Case managers in these settings combine the role of caregiver with case manager. The case manager may have hands-on nursing responsibilities.

- Liaise with providers
- Communicate with treating physicians
- Provide patient and family education
- Assess for and coordinate additional services and durable medical equipment (DME)
- Provide skilled nursing care

6. Workers' compensation organizations
Case management in workers' compensation cases focuses on vocational activities, such as collaborating with the employer to get the employee back to work.

- Facilitate communication between the employer, claims adjuster, attorneys, union representative, state administrative agency, and providers
- Coordinate care between multiple healthcare providers
- Monitor progress
- Utilization review
- Obtain precertification when necessary
- Perform job analysis
- Accompany injured workers during physician appointments

Goals and Objectives of Case Management Practice

Goals and objectives of case management include:

- Achieving client goals
- Client autonomy
- Client knowledge of disease process, prognosis, and treatment options
- Optimum health and functioning for the client
- Client ability to self-advocate
- Informed decision-making by the client
- Appropriate use of services and resources
- Timeliness of services
- Quality of care
- Appropriate level of care to meet client needs
- Optimal level of client independence
- Achieving optimal outcomes

Negotiation Techniques

Managed care contracts have decreased the need for price negotiations between case managers and providers, as pricing is set in advance. Even so, negotiating cost is still required in some situations, such as when services are not covered by the managed care contract or when working with out-of-network providers. Case managers may negotiate for services, such as length of stay, approval of needed services, and extra-contractual benefits.

What is negotiation, and how can case managers use it effectively?

Negotiation is the reaching of an agreement through discussion and compromise. The aim of negotiation is to explore the situation and find a mutually acceptable solution. There are two types of negotiation: aggressive/hardball and cooperative.

Aggressive or hardball negotiation aims to result in a winner and a loser. Tactics include intimidation, manipulation, tricks, and ridicule. The aggressive negotiator makes few concessions but extreme demands. He or she may threaten to cease negations. This type of negotiation often fails to reach an agreement. It results in mistrust and damages future negotiations. It is not recommended for case managers, as it can result in deadlock, leaving the patient without needed services.

Cooperative negotiation seeks a win-win outcome and usually results in the best end for everyone. The negotiator is trustworthy, objective, fair, and reasonable. This approach results in agreements faster and more often than the aggressive technique and facilitates future negotiations.

The Negotiation Process

Key to the negotiation process is being prepared, developing a relationship with the other party, and establishing a common ground in the best interest of the client. Showing respect for the other party can be as simple as returning voice mail or email promptly. The respect builds trust, which will enhance the negotiation process.

Communication is as important as respect in the negotiation process. It includes not only what you say, but also how you say it and how well you listen. In face-to-face communication, it also includes body language. Be clear and concise, and engage in active listening by paying attention (rather than planning how you will respond). Summarize the other person's comments and ask questions to clarify and ensure you understand his or her points.

Negotiation starts with preparation, so conduct research to understand the other person's side before meeting. (If negotiating price, know competitors' pricing.) Next, establish the problems and the goals with the other party. Failure to agree upon goals can make the negotiation process difficult.

Once the goals are established, determine what areas you agree on—these can be put aside—and what areas you disagree on. On the areas where there is disagreement, begin to work toward compromise. The negotiation is deemed successful when a mutually acceptable resolution is obtained.

The case manager can use negotiation effectively with patients, caregivers, and physicians, as well as payers and vendors. Once relationships are built, subsequent negotiations will be smoother and more enjoyable.

Case managers use negotiation to:

- Develop a realistic plan of care with patients and care providers
- Obtain approval for needed services
- Control cost
- Obtain benefits outside of the benefit contract
- Determine length of stay

Physical Functioning and Behavioral Health Assessment

The Activities of Daily Living (ADLs) and the more advanced Instrumental Activities of Daily Living (IADLs) are assessment tools that evaluate areas of essential function for self-care and independence.

ADLs measure the level of independence on performing six basic activities:

- Bathing
- Dressing
- Toileting/continence
- Transferring
- Hygiene/grooming
- Feeding

The ADLs can be easily remembered by the mnemonic DEATH: Dressing/bathing, Eating, Ambulating, Toileting, Hygiene.

The IADLs tool assesses the ability to perform eight independent living skills that are more complex than the basic ADLs assessment. These include:

- Shopping
- Using the telephone
- Paying bills/budgeting
- Food preparation
- Housekeeping
- Laundry
- Using transportation
- Handling medications

The Patient Health Questionnaire-2 (PHQ-2) pre-screens for depression. Clients who pre-screen positive for depression should be evaluated further with the Patient Health Questionnaire-9 (PHQ-9), which is the most common screening tool to identify depression. It asks the patient to rate the frequency of nine problems occurring over the previous two weeks on a scale ranging from 0 (not at all) to 3 (nearly every day), including little interest or pleasure in doing things, and feeling down, depressed, or hopeless.

Management of Acute and Chronic Illness and Disability

Acute diseases are characterized by rapid onset with a short duration. Appendicitis, flu, pneumonia, acute respiratory distress syndrome, and acute renal failure are examples of acute illnesses. In contrast, chronic diseases require a lifetime of management, such as diabetes, lupus, heart failure, and chronic renal failure.

An acute disease may lead to a chronic disease. Take, for example, a patient with acute onset of multisystem organ failure requiring a ventilator and dialysis.

If the patient is unable to wean from the ventilator or if kidney function does not return, the patient has developed a chronic condition.

In managing a patient with acute illness, the case manager should assess whether the patient will be able to return to his prior living arrangement. The case manager will also assess for any needs the patient may have upon discharge, such as home health care or durable medical equipment. If the patient is unable to return home directly from the hospital, the case manager facilitates transfer to inpatient rehabilitation, a long-term acute care hospital, or other suitable facility.

Patients with chronic disease must be taught to manage their condition to prevent morbidities and comorbidities. This includes medication management, lifestyle and dietary changes, and testing and follow-up with their healthcare provider. They must be educated on the benefits of treatment and the risks of noncompliance. They must understand that chronic diseases will not be cured, but rather managed, so they have better quality of life.

Acute illness, chronic illness, and disability are all disruptions to the patient's and family's lifestyle. Family members may have to take on additional responsibilities and rely on support systems. The case manager may make referrals to support groups or counselors, financial resources, or disease-based agencies.

Management of Clients with Multiple Chronic Illnesses

Many patients today have multiple comorbidities. As a result, these patients often receive care and information from multiple providers and care settings. This can lead to information overload and confusion about their treatment plans as they learn how to manage multiple conditions. Treatments should be coordinated by a single provider or a team that understands the patient's complex care needs.

Patients with multiple comorbidities are typically prescribed medications from multiple providers, leading to overmedication or medication interactions. For this reason, the case manager should review all medications upon opening the case, after each hospitalization, and after each visit to the doctor's office, at a minimum.

See section on Medication Therapy Management and Reconciliation for more information.

The case manager should also screen for medication compliance. There are numerous reasons for noncompliance, but one common reason in patients with comorbidities is cost. These patients have significant healthcare needs and therefore high healthcare costs. The out-of-pocket cost of their care, including the cost for prescription drugs, can be devastating. If this is the case, the case manager can suggest the patient explore several options:

- Medication samples from the doctor's office
- Generic drugs when appropriate
- Co-pay assistance programs
- Disease-specific financial assistance

When multiple comorbidities are present, it can be difficult to know where to start. In some cases, one condition is extremely critical or complex, making it obvious where to start. Examples include a recent diagnosis of cancer, end-stage disease, or a severely symptomatic disease. In the absence of a clinically dominant condition, however, concordant conditions are a good place to start. These conditions have the same overall pathophysiologic risk profile and are more likely to require similar management plans. An example of concordant conditions is hypertension, coronary artery disease, peripheral vascular disease, and diabetes.

At times, one disease complicates the management of other comorbid conditions. In these cases, this disease must be brought under control before other conditions can be successfully dealt with. For example, a patient who is severely depressed may not be able to make lifestyle changes or even keep doctor appointments. In this case, the first step is to treat the depression.

If none of the above circumstances apply, it is best to start where the patient feels most likely to have success. Patients can be easily overwhelmed by all the information available to them. Instead of providing all the handouts, pamphlets, and booklets at once, ask patients what information they would like to start with. Additional handouts can be added with each interaction.

No matter where you start, remember that patients with multiple comorbidities often require numerous lifestyle changes, as well as dietary changes or restrictions. It is often overwhelming for the patient to work on everything at once. To start, identify no more than 2-3 initial goals that the patient feels he or she can accomplish. Then, commend even the smallest achievements and focus on what the patient is doing right. This will build a foundation for future success.

Adherence to Care Regimen

Depending on the disease, it is estimated that 40-70% of patients do not adhere to their care regimen. Nonadherence means not carrying out the treatment plan or carrying it out incorrectly, and includes the failure to keep appointments, follow lifestyle changes, maintain dietary changes, and take medication as prescribed.

It is estimated that the cost of nonadherence is $100-300 billion annually. In addition to the financial implications there are clinical implications, such as decreased quality of life and premature death. An important task case managers perform is monitoring for and increasing patient adherence to care regimens.

Poor adherence to the care regimen leads to:
- Decreased quality of life
- Higher healthcare costs
- Increased emergency department visits
- Increased hospitalizations
- Avoidable nursing home admissions

- Decreased productivity
- Poor clinical outcomes
- Premature death

Conversely, improved patient adherence leads to better health outcomes, better chronic care management, improved population health, improved quality of life and productivity, and lower healthcare costs. Patient adherence is especially important for the long-term management of chronic diseases, such as kidney disease, heart disease, and diabetes.

There are numerous reasons for patient nonadherence, both intentional and unintentional. In some cases the patient feels the care regimen is too bothersome, complex, or unnecessary. In other instances there may be poor communication between the patient and the healthcare provider, or poor health literacy leading to misunderstanding of the care regimen. It is also not uncommon for patients to forget portions of what they were told by the provider. The medical industry is becoming increasingly complex, often leading to complex treatment plans. The more complex the treatment plan, the less likely a patient will adhere to it.

The case manager can increase adherence to the care regimen in several ways. The first is to assess the client's knowledge and understanding of his condition and care regimen. A patient's adherence can be directly correlated to his understanding.

Next, the case manager should get to know the client and develop a trusting relationship with him. Especially when dealing with complex care regimens, client knowledge alone is not enough to increase adherence. Understanding the client's beliefs, attitudes, support system, and self-efficacy will help the case manager communicate with the client and foster collaboration.

Once the case manager has a better understanding of what the client needs to know and what will motivate the client to adhere to the care regimen, she can begin to educate the client. For effective education:

- Use simple language, avoiding medical jargon
- Limit instructions to 3-4 major points during each discussion
- Supplement teaching with written materials when appropriate
- Involve the client's family or caregiver
- Evaluate client understanding
- Reinforce concepts previously taught

For clients with complex care regimens, case managers can use the Health Belief Model to optimize behavior change and adherence by ensuring that clients:

- Perceive themselves to be at risk due to lack of adoption of healthy behavior (perceived susceptibility)
- Perceive their medical conditions to be serious (perceived severity)
- Believe in the positive effects of the suggested treatment (perceived benefits)
- Have channels to address their fears and concerns (perceived barriers)
- Perceive themselves as having the requisite skills to perform the health behavior (self-efficacy)

By understanding which of these beliefs is lacking, the case manager can tailor interventions to meet the needs of the client.

Medication Adherence

According to a 2005 article published by the National Institutes of Health, studies show that nonadherence to medications causes 125,000 deaths annually and accounts for 10-25% of hospital and nursing home admissions in the United States. Overall, nearly 75% of adults are nonadherent in one or more ways.

The consequences of medication nonadherence are vast. Not only does the patient fail to benefit from the effects of the medication, but when the prescribing physician assumes that the patient is taking the medication as prescribed, he or she may make inappropriate medication, dosage, or treatment plan changes, which can result in further complications or adverse health outcomes. Creating a new illness is also a risk; for example, antibiotic-resistant bacteria came about due to patients not completing their courses of antibiotics.

Nonadherence to medications takes many forms, including primary nonadherence, such as not filling the prescription, and secondary nonadherence, such as not taking the prescription as prescribed (e.g., changing the dosage or frequency, stopping before completing the course of therapy, filling the prescription but never taking the medication, skipping or missing doses, or not refilling the prescription).

Factors that negatively affect adherence include:
- Side effects
- High copays or costs
- No noticeable symptoms of the disease (for example, hypercholesterolemia and hypertension do not produce noticeable symptoms)
- Multiple doses per day

To increase medication adherence, the case manager should first understand why the client is nonadherent. For example, if side effects are a problem, the solution could be to take the medication with food or to change the time of day it is taken. The client or case manager should discuss with the prescribing physician the inability to take the medication. An alternative medication may be prescribed, or one that counteracts the side effects.

If the client often forgets to take his medication, alarms, text messages, medication boxes, apps, and other reminders may help, or he could associate it with something in his daily routine, such as eating breakfast, going to bed, or brushing his teeth.

Reducing the number of pills or the frequency they are taken can also increase adherence. The physician may be able to prescribe a combination medication and/or extended release medication to decrease the number of pills taken.

Finally, educating the client can increase adherence. Clients who understand the purpose and importance of the prescription are more likely to be adherent.

Medication Therapy Management and Reconciliation

As defined by the Joint Commission on Accreditation of Health Care Organizations (JCAHO), medication reconciliation is "the process of comparing a patient's medication orders to all of the medications that the patient has been taking," to include name, dosage, route, and frequency. Medications should also be checked for compatibility.

A case manager will rarely have a client who is not taking any medications. It is much more likely a client is taking multiple medications, for multiple conditions, prescribed by multiple providers. It is important to review all prescribed medications, as well as over the counter medications and supplements, the patient is taking.

As discussed in the previous section, the case manager should assess the client's understanding of why he or she is prescribed the medications and how to take them properly, as well as the client's compliance with taking the medications as ordered. When the reason for noncompliance is identified, the case manager should notify the prescribing doctor and assist the patient with strategies to become compliant.

The goal of medication reconciliation is to decrease adverse drug events by reducing medication errors, such as omission, duplication, drug interactions, and dosing errors. Most errors occur during patient transitions in care, including changes in setting, level of care, or practitioner.

When Should Medication Reconciliation Occur?

- Any time the patient is moved within the hospital, such as from the ICU to the step down unit
- Upon transfer to another facility
- Upon discharge from any facility
- At each doctor office visit

Case managers should perform medication reconciliation upon opening the case, after each hospitalization, and after each visit to the doctor's office, at a minimum.

Transitions of Care/Transitional Care

Transitions of care can occur within a facility, such as when a patient is transferred from the ICU to the step down unit; between facilities, such as from a hospital to a skilled nursing facility; and within the community, from the primary care physician to the specialist.

A transitioning patient is at increased risk for an adverse outcome, due to medication errors, failure to follow up on testing or procedures, and/or not continuing prescribed treatments or therapies. Accountability—identifying who is responsible for what—is another concern. Failure to transition properly often occurs because of a communication breakdown. For this reason, the CMS recommends providers issue a summary of care for all transitions of care or referrals.

See Meaningful Use in the chapter Ethical, Legal and Practice Standards for more information.

The case manager is often involved during all points of transition and is in contact with the patient, family, and providers. This makes the case manager best suited to serve as coordinator of transitions of care.

Continuum of Care/Continuum of Health and Human Services

The continuum of care matches ongoing needs of the individuals being served by the case management process with the appropriate level and type of health, medical, financial, legal, and psychosocial care for services within a setting or across multiple settings.

The role of the case manager varies depending on where the patient is in the healthcare continuum. In a non-acute setting, the focus may be on preventing illness or deterioration of illness. If the patient is in the acute setting, the case manager will coordinate care and/or services.

A case manager's role is to ensure continuity of care when a patient transitions through the continuum of care. The case manager is in a unique position to make certain that appropriate information is communicated to multiple providers to ensure a safe transition.

Interdisciplinary Care Team

The Interdisciplinary Care Team (ICT) is a group of healthcare professionals from various professional disciplines who work together to manage the physical, psychological, and spiritual needs of the patient. Whenever possible the patient and the patient's family should be part of the team.

Members of the Interdisciplinary Care Team may include:

- Physicians
- Nurses
- Case manager
- Social worker
- Physical therapist

- Occupational therapist
- Chaplain
- Dietician
- Pharmacist

It is the hospital case manager's responsibility to assess the patient's post-hospital needs and resources available. When the needs are identified, the case manager facilitates referrals to appropriate community-based providers and services.

Healthcare Providers, Including Behavioral Health and Community Vendors

When referring a patient to a healthcare provider, the case manager should make sure the provider is professionally qualified to treat the patient. A "provider" is a person, such as a doctor or nurse, or a corporation or organization. Providers include:

- Acute care hospitals (and the services they provide, such as ED, ICU, transplant, OB)
- Long-term acute care hospitals
- Acute inpatient rehabilitation and any specialty rehabilitation facility (e.g., trauma, spinal cord, brain, stroke)
- Skilled nursing facility/Subacute care
- Urgent care
- Retail health clinics (e.g., CVS Minute Clinic)
- Home health
- Hospice (home and inpatient hospice)
- Physicians and specialists
- Nurse practitioners

- Certified nurse midwives
- Long-term care facilities and their specialties, such as Alzheimer's or dementia
- Assisted living
- Durable medical equipment providers
- Specialty supply companies
- Outpatient rehabilitation/Day programs
- Free and/or reduced cost medical clinics
- Certified psychiatric nurse specialists (who perform psychotherapy and manage medications)
- Behavioral health counselors (who perform counseling and psychotherapy services but cannot prescribe medication)
- Clinical psychologists (who perform psychotherapy and psychological testing and counseling but cannot prescribe medication)
- Psychiatrists (who treat people with more serious disturbances requiring medication, such as major depression, attention deficit disorder, and bipolar disorder; they also perform psychotherapy and manage medication)

Roles and Functions of Other Providers in Various Settings

Life Care Planner

Life care planning is a sub-specialty of case management and other professions. It provides a comprehensive care plan for the health needs of an individual who has experienced a catastrophic injury or has chronic healthcare needs. A life care planner completes a comprehensive assessment, data analysis, and research to provide an organized and concise plan for the present and future needs of an individual. Life care plans are used by:

- Attorneys, to determine future care cost for a client
- Treatment teams, to provide a plan for ongoing treatment and follow up
- Trust managers, to identify scheduled needs and associated costs
- Patients and families, to coordinate and facilitate resources

Vocational Case Manager

Vocational case managers assist employees to return to work as quickly as possible.

Physician

The role of the physician is to improve the health and well-being of individuals by promoting, maintaining, or restoring health through diagnosis and treatment. The physician evaluates symptoms, performs tests, and prescribes medication or treatment for an illness or injury. He or she also counsels patients on how to prevent illness.

Nurse Practitioner

A nurse practitioner (NP) is an advance practice nurse who helps with all aspects of patient care, including diagnosis, treatment, and consultations. In some states NPs can practice independently. Nurse practitioners can prescribe medications, including controlled substances, in all 50 states.

Certified Nurse Midwife

Certified nurse midwives care for childbearing women during preconception, prenatal, labor, delivery, and postpartum periods. They also provide family-planning counseling and gynecological care. They care for low-risk patients who desire a more natural and intervention-free childbirth experience.

Chiropractor

Chiropractors treat patients with health problems of the neuromusculoskeletal system, which includes nerves, bones, muscles, ligaments, and tendons. They use spinal adjustments, manipulation, and other techniques to manage patients' health concerns, such as back and neck pain.

Speech-Language Pathologist

A speech-language pathologist or speech-language therapist assesses, diagnoses, treats, and helps prevent disorders of speech, language, cognitive-communication, voice, swallowing, fluency, and other related areas.

Hospice, Palliative, and End of Life Care

Hospice provides end of life care, including palliative care, to patients with terminal illness. Hospice also supports the patient's family. To qualify for hospice care, a physician must document that the patient has a terminal illness that reduces life expectancy and that the patient is near the end of life. Hospice care can be provided in the patient's home, in the hospital, or in a freestanding hospice facility. Hospice care is a covered benefit for Medicare, Medicaid in most states, most private insurance companies, and many HMOs. The case manager should check the individual's hospice benefit for private insurance and HMOs, as benefits will vary.

Medicare Hospice Benefit

Medicare patients who elect the hospice benefit have minimal to no out-of-pocket expenses for most hospice services. There is no deductible for hospice care. The only cost-sharing responsibilities come from a 5% coinsurance for inpatient respite care, if used, and a copayment of up to $5 per outpatient prescription drug.

The eligibility requirements for Medicare Hospice Benefit are:

- The patient has Medicare Part A.
- The hospice program is Medicare approved.

- The physician certifies that the patient has a life expectancy of six months or less if the illness runs its normal course.

- The patient must waive the normal Medicare hospital benefit to choose hospice care. This means that Medicare will not pay for hospitalization related to the terminal illness. For example, if a patient were admitted to hospice with a diagnosis of terminal pancreatic cancer, Medicare would not pay for a hospitalization for jaundice related to the pancreatic cancer. If, however, the patient fell and broke his hip, Medicare would cover that hospitalization.

Hospice care is given in benefit periods. The first and second benefit periods are 90 days each. These periods are followed by unlimited 60-day benefit periods. At the start of each benefit period, a physician must certify that the patient is terminally ill. The patient may change hospice providers once during a benefit period.

Medicare pays a daily rate based on level of care. The levels of care include:

- Routine home care (paid at a higher rate during the first 90-day benefit period than subsequent periods)
- Continuous home care
- Inpatient respite care
- General inpatient care

Medicaid Hospice Services

States are required to offer hospice benefits for at least 210 days. The Medicaid hospice program covers physician services provided by the hospice agency, nursing care, physical therapy, occupational therapy, speech therapy, social worker services, dietary counseling, medical equipment and supplies, medications for symptom control and pain relief, hospice aide and homemaker services, and short-term inpatient care for pain control, symptom management, and respite care.

Medicaid pays a daily rate based on the level of care, as Medicare does. Beginning March 23, 2010, with the enactment of the Affordable Care Act, Medicaid and Children's Health Insurance Program (CHIP) eligible individuals under age 21 who elect the hospice benefit no longer have to waive services for the cure or treatment of the terminal condition and can receive both curative care and hospice care for the terminal condition.

The eligibility requirements for hospice care under Medicaid are:
- Terminal illness certified by a physician
- Reduced life expectancy (stated by the physician) as defined by the state in which Medicaid is received
- Election of the hospice benefit
- Patient agrees to give up curative care in favor of care to manage symptoms and promote comfort, unless the patient is younger than 21 years of age

See the section titled End of Life Issues in the chapter Psychosocial Concepts and Support Systems for more information on Hospice and Palliative Care.

Financial Resources

The diagnosis of a serious or terminal illness can be financially devastating for an individual and his or her family. Often the patient can no longer work and the medical bills mount, quickly depleting a person's entire life savings. The following are financial resources that may be available.

Waiver Programs

Medicaid Waiver programs provide long-term care services at home and in the community to people who would otherwise be in an institution, nursing home, or hospital. Prior to the waivers, the federal Medicaid program only paid for long-term care services provided in an institution. Waiver programs can provide a combination of standard medical services and non-medical services. Standard services include but are not limited to: case management, homemaker, home health aide, personal care, adult day health services, habilitation (both day and residential), and respite care. States can also propose other services that may assist in diverting and/or transitioning individuals from institutional settings into their homes and communities.

Special Needs Trusts

A trust is a relationship between three parties: a donor who contributes the funds for the trust, a trustee who manages and administers the funds according to the donor's wishes, and a beneficiary who receives the funds. A special needs trust (SNT) is designed for beneficiaries who are disabled, either physically or mentally. SNTs can be tailored to meet the unique circumstances of each family.

Types of SNTs include General Support and Supplemental Care. The General Support SNT is designed to be the primary or sole source of benefits for the beneficiary. This type of trust is considered an available resource of the beneficiary and can make him or her ineligible for needs-based benefits. The Supplemental Care SNT is designed as a secondary source of benefits for the beneficiary after governmental benefits have been exhausted. A properly prepared Supplemental Care SNT will allow the beneficiary to be eligible for need-based government benefits, such as Medicaid and Supplemental Security Income, while still receiving funds from the trust.

Accelerated Death Benefit

Some life insurance policies have an accelerated death benefit (ADB) rider, allowing an insured person with a terminal illness to use some of the policy's benefit prior to dying. The ADB is deducted from the amount the beneficiaries receive at death. There are restrictions on how the money can be used; generally it can be used for long-term care and medical expenses.

Viatical Settlements

A life insurance policy is personal property, meaning it can be sold. A viatical settlement sells the life insurance policy of a person with a terminal or life-threatening illness and a life expectancy of less than five years to a third party for cash. There are no restrictions on how this money can be used. The purchasing party then becomes the beneficiary and takes responsibility for paying the premium.

The insured are normally paid between 50-80% of the face value of the policy. This amount is dependent on a number of factors, such as life expectancy, current interest rates, and the cost of paying the premium.

Due to HIPAA protections, the money received from a viatical settlement is usually free from federal income tax. On the other hand, earnings may impact eligibility for some means-based programs such as Medicaid.

Reverse Mortgages

A reverse mortgage may be an option for a patient who is a homeowner and age 62 or older. Under a reverse mortgage, the patient borrows against his or her home's value without having to leave the home or make payments. The funds can be distributed by:

- Lump sum
- Fixed monthly installments
- Line of credit

The payment structure of the proceeds may impact Medicaid eligibility. The line of credit is the most popular choice and often is not considered an asset when determining Medicaid eligibility.

The amount of money received through a reverse mortgage is determined by the home's value, the age of the borrower, and current interest rates. There are no restrictions on how the money can be used. The loan does not have to be repaid until the last borrower dies, sells the house, or moves out.

A reverse mortgage is not for everyone. Both spouses must be 62 or older to be listed on the reverse mortgage deed. If only one spouse is listed, and he or she dies first, the surviving spouse must repay the loan in full or be evicted.

Insurance Principles

Actuarial Study

An actuarial study is a statistical analysis of a population based on its utilization of healthcare services and demographic trends of the population. The results of this study are used to estimate healthcare plan premiums or costs. An actuary is a trained professional who specializes in determining policy rates, calculating premiums, and conducting statistical studies.

Appeal

An appeal is a formal process or request to reconsider a healthcare decision, such as denial of hospital admission or reimbursement for healthcare services. An appeal can also request to extend the length of a hospital stay. Insurance policies have differing appeal rights and processes; the following is a general overview:

> Peer-to-peer review – Not actually an appeal but rather a request by the treating physician for a discussion with the initial reviewer, to discuss the case and why it should not be denied.

> First level appeal – A request for an additional review of the decision to deny service. To meet 2005 Utilization Review Accreditation Commission (URAC) standards, the decision must be appealed by a physician who was not involved in the original denial.

External review – A review conducted by an independent review organization, typically after the insurance company's internal review process has been exhausted.

Extra-contractual Benefits

Extra-contractual benefits are benefits not covered under the health plan but are given to the insured due to the cost savings for the health insurance plan. For example, a patient in a skilled nursing facility for complex dressing changes, who has exhausted his home care benefit, would be allowed additional home care visits for dressing changes. In this case, discharging the patient from the more costly skilled nursing facility and providing the patient home care benefit beyond the contract limit will save the insurance company money.

Medical Necessity

Insurance will cover only healthcare that is medically necessary. What is deemed medically necessary varies by health plan. In general, medically necessary services are those that are reasonable, necessary, appropriate, and based on evidence-based standards of care.

Precertification

Precertification or preauthorization is the process of obtaining and documenting advanced approval from the health plan before the medical services occur. When planning the patient's care, the case manager should know if and when precertification is required.

Self-insured/Self-funded

Some employer groups choose to self-insure. These businesses pay employees' medical claims with their own funds, though they may purchase stop-loss insurance to protect themselves from extremely large healthcare costs. The stop-loss insurance takes over responsibility for paying claims after the self-insured company has paid a specified dollar amount in claims.

Self-funded companies may choose to contract with a TPA (third party administrator) or an ASO (administrative services only) to handle the administrative aspects of insurance, such as claims processing.

Coordination of Benefits (COB)

To prevent double payment for services when a subscriber has coverage from two or more sources, the National Association of Insurance Commissioners created COB guidelines. Following these guidelines is not mandatory, but most states and commercial insurances choose to use these COB provisions to determine which insurer is primary and which is secondary.

The primary plan is initially responsible for payment of benefits for covered services as if there were no other plan. After the primary plan has paid, the balance is passed to the secondary company, which pays according to its contract.

The following determines which plan is primary:
- Medicaid always pays last.
- If an insurance plan does not have a COB provision, it must pay primary.
- If none of the below apply, the coverage that has been in force the longest is primary.

Employees
- The insurance plan covering the client as an employee is the primary payer over a plan covering the individual as a dependent, which pays secondary.
- The insurance plan that covers an active employee is primary over the plan that covers a retiree or laid-off employee.
- The insurance plan that covers an active employee is primary over a COBRA plan, which is secondary.

Dependents of married parents
- If the parents are married, the birthday rules states that the parent whose birthday comes first in the year is primary for the children.

Dependents of non-married parents
- If the parents are not married and both plans cover the client as a dependent, primary coverage is determined by the court.
- If no court determination has been made, the parent with custody is primary, followed by the spouse of the parent with custody, and finally the parent without custody.

Medicare
- Age 65 or older and retired, Medicare is primary.
- Age 65 or older and covered due to the patient or his spouse working for an employer with 20 or more employees, the employer plan is primary.
- Age 65 or older and covered due to patient or spouse working for employer with fewer than 20 employees, Medicare is primary.

Disability

Workers' compensation, short-term disability insurance (STD), long-term disability insurance (LTD), and Social Security Disability Insurance (SSDI) benefits all provide financial compensation for workers who are unable to work. There are differences between the programs, however. Workers' compensation only covers work-related injuries, while STD and LTD cover loss of work due to illness, injury, or accident that is not work-related.

Workers' compensation provides replacement of lost wages and a medical benefit for the work-related injury. STD and LTD only cover a portion of the wages, typically 50-70%, and begin after a waiting period.

Workers' compensation is mandated to be paid by the employer. The employer can also provide LTD and STD as part of a benefits package, or an individual can purchase LTD and/or STD policies from an agent. LTD purchased from an agent is not taxed, whereas LTD as part of a benefits package is taxed. SSDI is paid for by a tax on the employer and the employee.

Disability Comparison

	WC	STD	LTD	SSDI
Wage Replacement	Yes	Yes, a portion	Yes, a portion	Yes, amount depends on work record
Medical Benefit	Yes	No	No	Medicare is available after 24 months of receiving SSDI
Work Related	Yes	Covers non-work related injury, accident, or illness	Covers non-work related injury, accident, or illness	Covers non-work related injury, accident, or illness
Paid By	Employer	Employer, employee, or both	Employer, employee, or both	Funded by Social Security taxes paid by workers, employers, and the self-employed
Waiting Period	No	Yes, usually 7-30 days (and ends 90-180 days after day of disability)	Yes, LTD usually begins after STD ends	5-month waiting period

Workers' Compensation

Workers' compensation laws protect employees who are injured or disabled on the job. They are designed to provide fixed monetary awards, eliminating the need for litigation. Workers covered by workers' compensation cannot sue their employer for work-related injuries. Benefits include both medical costs and lost wages and are awarded to the worker regardless of who was at fault for the accident.

The employer is 100% responsible for paying for workers' compensation insurance. The employer is also responsible for filing the First Report of Injury with the insurance carrier and the state workers' compensation agency, if required. In addition to covering injured and disabled workers, workers' compensation also provides benefits for dependents of workers killed by work-related accidents or illnesses.

Workers' compensation regulations vary from state to state, and state mandates take precedence over the financial status or will of the employer. Federal statutes are limited to federal employees or those workers employed in some significant aspect of interstate commerce.

Federal Workers' Compensation Programs

Federal Employment Compensation Act – Provides workers' compensation for non-military federal employees.

Federal Employment Liability Act (FELA) – Ensures that railroads engaged in interstate commerce are liable for injuries to their employees if they have been negligent.

Merchant Marine Act (aka the Jones Act) – Provides seamen with the same protection from employer negligence as FELA provides for railroad workers.

Longshore and Harbor Workers' Compensation Act (LHWCA) – Provides workers' compensation to specified employees of private maritime employers.

Black Lung Benefits Act – Provides compensation for miners suffering from "black lung." The Act requires liable mine operators to pay disability payments. It also establishes a fund that provides disability payments to miners when the mine operator is unknown or unable to pay.

Workers' compensation pays for:

- Medical care that is considered "reasonable and customary" for work-related injuries, beginning immediately after the injury occurs
- Temporary disability benefits
- Permanent partial and permanent total disability benefits to workers who have lasting consequences of disabilities caused on the job
- Rehabilitation and training benefits for those unable to return to pre-injury careers
- Benefits to survivors of workers who die of work-related causes

Claims Management Strategies

Workers' compensation always pays primary to short-term disability (STD), long-term disability (LTD), and Social Security Disability Insurance (SSDI).

When considering the award amount for loss of income or earning capacity due to an occupational injury, disease, or death, the following classifications of disability are used:

- Temporary Total Disability (TTD) – The worker is totally incapacitated for work beyond the day on which the accident occurred but is subsequently able to return to work. The majority of workers' compensation injuries fall under this classification.
- Permanent Total Disability (PTD) – The injury permanently and totally incapacitates the injured worker from carrying out gainful employment.

- Temporary Partial Disability (TPD) – The worker is partially incapacitated for the length of the disability. Although unable to perform normal work duties, he or she may engage in modified work.
- Permanent Partial Disability (PPD) – The worker has a partial loss of function that does not prevent work and is permanent.

Long-Term Care Insurance

Traditional insurance and Medicare do not pay for long-term care (LTC). A long-term care policy may offset some or all of the cost of long-term care. These policies vary widely, but usually have a limit on the dollar amount or number of years one can receive the benefit.

Some policies cover care in the patient's home, while others only cover care in a facility. Depending on the LTC company, the patient may be able to hire independent providers or family members to care for them. Other companies require the patient use a certified agency or licensed providers. Some of the services that may be covered include: adult daycare, home care, home modifications, assisted living, and nursing home.

Private Benefit Programs

Employer-sponsored Health Coverage

Employer-sponsored health insurance is coverage offered by an employer to its employees. Employers can choose to purchase a fully-insured plan and pay a fixed premium to an insurance carrier, or to self-insure the health plan. With a fully-insured plan the premium cost is set for the year. The insurance carrier collects the premium and pays the claims as outlined in the policy.

Some employers choose to self-fund their health plans in an attempt to reduce costs. Self-funded, or self-insured, employers do not pay a fixed premium to an insurance carrier. Instead they pay for each claim as it is incurred, out of pocket.

To do this, they must meet the state legal and financial requirements.

Self-insured employers may purchase reinsurance, excess risk, or stop-loss insurance to offset very large claims. Employers that self-insure often contract with third party administrators (TPAs) or administrative services only (ASOs) to handle the administrative aspects of insurance, such as utilization review and processing claims. Self-funded plans are regulated federally by ERISA (Employee Retirement Income Security Act of 1974) and are exempt from most laws regulating fully-insured plans on the state level.

Individual-purchased Insurance

Individual health insurance is purchased on an individual or family basis, as opposed to being provided by the employer. Individual health insurance policies are regulated by the state in which they are purchased. The Affordable Care Act (ACA) has made significant changes to how individual policies are rated and the benefits that these policies provide. All policies must cover the same set of Essential Health Benefits. The ACA also subsidizes policies purchased through the exchanges for certain qualified individuals.

Indemnity

CCMC defines indemnity benefits as "benefits in the form of payments rather than services." In most cases, this means the healthcare provider bills the patient, and the insurance company reimburses the patient later. Indemnity benefits are also known as fee-for-service. The patient is free to choose his or her provider without restriction, but indemnity policies are more expensive than managed care policies.

Pharmacy Benefit Management

Pharmacy benefit management services use a number of strategies to control the cost of prescription medications. One such strategy is contracting with a network of retail pharmacies to provide discounted rates for members. They may also use mail order pharmacies, through which medications are mailed to the patient's home at a savings over retail prices. Pharmacy benefit management services use their large purchasing power to negotiate discounts from drug manufacturers. They also develop and maintain a formulary—a list of drugs approved for reimbursement—to encourage the use of lower cost drugs. Pharmacy benefit management services often use payment tiers, with generic drugs being the cheapest, followed by formulary medications, and then non-formulary medications.

Home Care Benefits

Most benefit plans include home care. The extent of the benefit varies, so the case manager should be aware of the limitations on this benefit. There may be limits on the number of visits per year, the number of hours per visit, and/or the types of services that may be provided.

COBRA

In 1986, Congress passed the Consolidated Omnibus Budget Reconciliation Act (COBRA). Under this law, employees and their families who might otherwise lose their health insurance due to job loss, decreased work hours, transition between jobs, death, divorce, and other life events, can choose to keep their insurance. Employers (private sector or state/local government) with 20 or more employees offer COBRA.

If a person elects COBRA coverage, he continues to receive group health benefits from the plan for a limited period of time. The duration of coverage under COBRA is usually 18 months but can last up to 36 months under certain circumstances. In the event of death of the employee or legal separation or divorce from the employee, the spouse and dependent children are eligible to receive COBRA coverage for 36 months. If the employee or eligible dependent is qualified to receive COBRA due to termination or reduction of hours, and then becomes disabled on or prior to day 60 of COBRA, he is eligible for 29 months of coverage.

The eligible person must elect COBRA within 60 days of the plan coverage terminating. After the initial election, the first premium payment must be made within 45 days. After this, payments are due on the first of each month, subject to a 30-day grace period. If payments are not made as stated, coverage may be terminated.

A person receiving COBRA benefits may be required to pay the entire premium (including the portion previously paid by the employer), as well as a 2% fee. Thus, COBRA may cost up to 102% of the plan's premium, putting COBRA financially out of reach for many of the people who qualify for it.

Public Benefit Programs

Public benefits programs include Social Security Disability Insurance (SSDI), Supplemental Security Income (SSI), Medicare, and Medicaid. Individuals who are entitled to both Medicare and Medicaid are called dual eligibles. In the case of dual eligibles, Medicaid always pays last.

Medicare

Medicare is health insurance provided by the U.S. Government for people who are 65 or older, certain younger people with disabilities, and people with End Stage Renal Disease (ESRD). It was created in 1966 under Title XVIII of the Social Security Act and is administered by Centers for Medicare & Medicaid Services (CMS). Medicare covers some but not all medical costs and pays under the Prospective Payment System (PPS) for most care settings. Medicare eligibility is not based on income.

Eligibility for Medicare benefits:

- 65 or older, or
- Have a specific long-term disability (and have been receiving Social Security Disability benefits for at least 24 months), or
- Have Lou Gehrig's disease (the waiting period is also waived), or
- Diagnosed with permanent kidney failure (ESRD), requiring dialysis or transplant

Medicare has 4 parts:

- Part A (Hospital Insurance)
- Part B (Medical Insurance)
- Part C (Medicare Advantage Plan)
- Part D (Prescription Drugs)

Medicare Part A

Medicare Part A pays for:

- Inpatient hospital stays, including acute care hospitals, critical access hospitals, inpatient rehabilitation facilities, and long-term care hospitals
- Skilled nursing facility stays
- Some home health care
- Hospice care

Some individuals must pay a premium for Medicare Part A, but most people are covered for free. To be eligible for premium-free Part A, an individual must be entitled to receive Medicare based on their own earnings or those of a spouse, parent, or child. The worker must have a specified number of quarters of coverage (QCs). The exact number or QCs required depends on whether the person is filing for Part A coverage on the basis of age, disability, or ESRD. QCs are earned through payment of payroll taxes under the Federal Insurance Contributions Act (FICA) during the person's working years.

To be eligible for premium Part A, an individual must be age 65 or older and be enrolled in Medicare Part B.

Inpatient Hospital Coverage Under Medicare

Medicare covers up to 90 days of medically necessary inpatient hospital care per benefit period. The beneficiary is responsible for the initial deductible and a copayment based on when in the benefit period they are hospitalized.

Benefit Periods

- A benefit period begins when the beneficiary is first admitted to the hospital. It ends when the patient has been out of the hospital or skilled nursing facility for at least 60 consecutive days.
- There is no limit to the number of benefit periods covered during a beneficiary's lifetime.
- Inpatient hospital care is normally limited to 90 days during a benefit period.
- Copayment is required for days 61-90.
- If the 90 days are exhausted, the beneficiary can elect to use days from a non-renewable "lifetime reserve" of up to 60 additional days of inpatient hospital care. (Copayment is also required for these days.)

Skilled Nursing Facility (SNF) Coverage Under Medicare

- Only covered if it follows within 30 days of a hospital stay of 3 days or more and is medically necessary
- Limited to 100 days per benefit period
- Copayment required for days 21-100
- Custodial care not covered

Home Health Care Under Medicare Part A

- Covers first 100 visits following 3-day hospitalization or SNF stay
- No copay or deductible

- Home health aide is covered for homebound member, if intermittent or part time skilled nursing and/or other therapy or rehabilitation is provided
- Full time nursing is not covered

Medicare Hospice Coverage

- Terminally ill with a life expectancy of six months or less
- Relinquish standard Medicare benefits for the treatment of illness
- If patient requires treatment for a condition not related to his or her terminal illness, Medicare will pay for services for that condition
- No deductible
- Small coinsurance for drugs and inpatient respite care

Medicare Part B

Medicare Part B is voluntary insurance; there is a monthly premium for coverage.

It pays for:

- Physician and surgeon services
- Outpatient services
- Some home health care
- Durable medical equipment
- Emergency room care
- Preventive services
- Ambulance services

Medicare Part B covers home health care not associated with a hospital or SNF stay. It also covers after the 100 days covered under Part A. There is no copayment or deductible for home health. Durable medical equipment requires a 20% coinsurance.

Medicare Part C (Medicare Advantage Plan)

Managed care option to obtain coverage for Parts A and B and sometimes D, through a private health plan such as an HMO, PPO, Special Needs Plan, private fee-for-service plan, or Medicare Medical Savings Account plan

- Plans contract with the government to administer Medicare benefits to members
- Plans are required to provide services covered in Medicare Parts A and B except hospice
- There is a monthly premium

Medicare Part D

Provides subsidized access to prescription drug coverage on a voluntary basis

- Participants pay a premium
- Covers most FDA-approved prescription drugs

Supplemental Policies

Private insurance companies offer supplemental policies known as Medigap to help cover Medicare's out-of-pocket expenses.

Medicaid

Medicaid is a health insurance program funded jointly by the states and the federal government for individuals with limited income and resources. Medicaid also covers services not normally covered by Medicare, such as long-term support and services, as well as personal care services.

Eligibility

The Affordable Care Act created a national Medicaid minimum eligibility level of 133% of the federal poverty level for nearly all Americans under the age of 65. Other non-financial eligibility criteria are used in determining Medicaid eligibility. Coverage can be retroactive up to three months prior to the month of application if the individual would have been eligible during the retroactive period. Medicaid eligibility varies from state to state, but in general covers limited income individuals in the following categories:

- People 65 or older
- Children under 19
- Pregnant women
- Disabled individuals
- A parent caring for a child
- An eligible immigrant

Medicaid Benefits

States establish and administer their Medicaid programs. They also determine the type, amount, duration, and scope of services, within the federal guidelines. States are required to cover certain "mandatory benefits" and can choose to provide "optional benefits." Generally speaking, Medicaid covers:

- Doctors visits
- Hospital stays
- Long-term services and supports (e.g., institutional care, home care, community-based long-term services)
- Preventive care, including immunizations, mammograms, and colonoscopies
- Prenatal and maternity care
- Mental health care
- Necessary medications
- Vision and dental care for children

Asset Considerations Related to Medicaid

Spousal Impoverishment: The expenses of nursing home care can rapidly deplete the savings of couples. In 1988 Congress enacted provisions to prevent what has come to be called "spousal impoverishment"—that is, when the spouse still living at home has little or no income or resources. Under the Medicaid spousal impoverishment provisions, a certain amount of the couple's combined resources is protected when one spouse enters a nursing facility or other medical institution and is expected to remain there for at least 30 days.

Treatment of Trusts: When an individual, his or her spouse, or anyone acting on the individual's behalf establishes a trust using at least some of the individual's funds, that trust can be considered available to the individual for purposes of determining eligibility for Medicaid.

Transfers of Assets for Less Than Fair Market Value: This practice is prohibited for the purposes of establishing Medicaid eligibility. It applies when assets are transferred, sold, or gifted for less than they are worth by individuals in long-term care facilities or receiving home and community-based waiver services, by their spouses, or by someone else acting on their behalf.

Estate Recovery: State Medicaid programs must recover from a Medicaid enrollee's estate the cost of certain benefits paid on behalf of the enrollee. These benefits include: nursing facilities services, home and community-based services, and related hospital and prescription drug services.

SSDI

Social Security Disability Insurance, or SSDI, is an earned benefit, like the Social Security retirement benefit. It is given to those unable to work due to disability based on physical or mental impairment. To be eligible for SSDI, an individual must be unable to perform the work they previously did and not be able to adjust to other work because of the condition. The disability must be expected to last for at least one year or to result in death. At age 65 the benefit automatically converts to the retirement benefit, but the benefit amount remains the same.

Overview of SSDI:

- Based on work record
- Funded by Social Security taxes paid by workers, employers, and the self-employed
- For those over age 18 and under 65
- Covers blind or disabled workers
- Focuses on physical and mental impairments severe enough to prevent engaging in normal occupation or any other work
- A 5-month waiting period for benefits to begin
- Approval for SSDI can come quickly if the individual has one of the serious medical conditions named on the Social Security Compassionate Allowance List; otherwise obtaining SSDI approval is a long process
- After receiving SSDI for 24 months, an individual is eligible for Medicare; including the 5-month waiting period, this equals 29 months before Medicare eligibility
- Like the Social Security retirement benefit, it can be paid to children, widows/widowers, and adults who haven't worked but have been disabled since childhood

SSI

Supplemental Security Income (SSI) is a need-based program that makes cash assistance payments to disabled individuals with limited income and resources. SSI is financed by general revenues collected by the Treasury Department. The disability criteria are the same as for SSDI. Individuals eligible for SSI are also eligible for Medicaid.

Benefit types:

- Age (65 and older)
- Disability (any age, includes children)
- Blindness (any age, includes children)

Comparison of Public Benefit Programs

	Medicare	Medicaid	SSDI	SSI
Benefit Type	Medical	Medical	Cash Benefit	Cash Benefit
Benefits based on	Earnings	Need	Earnings	Need
Financed by	Employer and wage contributions	General Revenues	Employer and wage contributions	General Revenues
Income/ Resource Limit for Eligibility	No limit	Income and resource limits	No limit	Income and resource limits
Work Credits Required	Yes	No	Yes	No
Basis for Benefit Amount	N/A	N/A	Average lifetime earnings	Federal and state laws

Military Benefit Programs

TRICARE

TRICARE is the healthcare program for service members (active, Guard/Reserve, and retired) and their families. It was formerly known as the Civilian

Health and Medical Program of the Uniformed Services (CHAMPUS). TRICARE is managed by the Defense Health Agency (DHA) and uses military healthcare as its main delivery system, supported by a civilian network of providers and facilities.

TRICARE offers three basic options for care:

- TRICARE Prime: an HMO type plan
- TRICARE Extra: a PPO type plan
- TRICARE Standard: a fee-for-service plan

Other TRICARE benefits:

- TRICARE for Life – Medicare wraparound coverage for beneficiaries entitled to Medicare
- TRICARE Reserve Select – Coverage for National Guard and Reserve members
- TRICARE Retired Reserve – Coverage for Retired National Guard and Reserve Members and their families
- TRICARE Young Adult – Allows qualified dependent adult children to purchase coverage up to age 26 after their regular coverage ends
- Continued Health Care Benefit Program (CHCBP) – Temporary transitional healthcare coverage for 18-36 months after TRICARE benefits end
- TRICARE pharmacy program
- TRICARE dental program

VA

The Veterans Health Administration is America's largest integrated healthcare system with over 1,700 sites of care, serving 8.76 million veterans each year. Veterans of the United States Uniformed Services may be eligible for a broad range of programs and services provided by the Department of Veterans Affairs (VA). VA Health Benefits include all the necessary inpatient hospital care and outpatient services to promote, preserve, or restore health. VHA medical facilities provide a wide range of services, including traditional hospital-based services such as surgery, critical care, mental health, orthopedics, pharmacy, radiology, and physical therapy.

Eligibility for most VA benefits is based upon discharge from active military service under other than dishonorable conditions. Many veterans qualify for cost-free healthcare based on a service-connected condition or other qualifying factors. Some veterans may be required to pay a copay for treatment of their nonservice-connected conditions.

CHAMPVA

The Civilian Health and Medical Program of the Department of Veterans Affairs (CHAMPVA) is a comprehensive healthcare program in which the VA shares the cost of covered healthcare services, supplies, and pharmaceuticals with eligible beneficiaries. Due to the similarity between CHAMPVA and the Department of Defense (DoD) TRICARE program (previously known as CHAMPUS), the two are often confused. CHAMPVA is a Department of Veterans Affairs program; TRICARE is a regionally managed healthcare program for active duty and retired members of the uniformed services, their families, and survivors. In general, CHAMPVA covers most healthcare services and supplies that are medically and psychologically necessary.

TRICARE For Life

TRICARE For Life (TFL) is Medicare wraparound coverage for TRICARE beneficiaries who have Medicare Part A and Medicare Part B. It provides comprehensive healthcare coverage. Medicare is the primary payer. Beneficiaries can receive care from any Medicare participating or Medicare nonparticipating provider as well as at any military clinic or hospital. If receiving services from a Medicare nonparticipating provider, TRICARE pays only the amount it would have paid if the beneficiary had gone to a Medicare participating provider (normally 20% of the TRICARE allowable charge).

Reimbursement and Payment Methodologies

The two main reimbursement categories for paying for healthcare are fee-for-service and episode-of-care. With fee-for-service reimbursement, each service rendered is priced separately. For example, mastectomy services would include charges for the hospital room, medications, surgical supplies, the OR suite, physician charges, surgeon charges, anesthesia, anesthesiologist, post-op office visits, and so on. With episode-of-care reimbursement, the episode is reimbursed in one lump sum, eliminating individual fees or charges.

It is believed by some in the medical community that the fee-for-service payment system encourages overuse of healthcare resources. The episode-of-care payment method attempts to correct this by paying one predetermined amount, no matter the number or cost of services provided.

Two types of episode-of-care reimbursement are bundled/case rates and the prospective payment system.

Bundled/Case Rate

The terms bundled and case rate are used interchangeably, though there are some subtle differences. Both make a single payment for all services related to a treatment or condition. The term bundled is used more often when referring to "bundling" physician and hospital charges or charges to multiple providers in multiple settings. Case rate is used when referring to a flat fee paid to the provider for a client's treatment based on his diagnosis or presenting problem.

In general, both terms represent a single comprehensive payment made to healthcare providers to cover all of the services the client requires for a specific treatment or condition. Bundled or case rates are often used in orthopedic procedures such as total hip replacements, cardiac procedures such as CABG (coronary artery bypass grafting), and maternity care.

Prospective Payment System

A Prospective Payment System (PPS) is a method of reimbursement in which payment is made based on a predetermined, fixed amount. The PPS was developed to motivate providers to deliver patient care in a cost-effective, efficient manner without over-utilization of services. Providers know how much they will be reimbursed by the insurance company in advance and can either make money or lose money on the reimbursement. Where the traditional fee-for-service payment system can create an incentive to add unnecessary services, the PPS system discourages this.

The PPS also encourages efficiency. Where a hospital may have kept a patient over the weekend to perform a test or procedure on Monday, the PPS system incentivizes the hospital to call in staff to conduct it over the weekend. This can lead to faster diagnosis and treatment, shorter hospital stays, and ultimately lower costs.

Medicare's Prospective Payment System

Medicare's PPS determines the payment amount for a particular service based on the classification system of that service. For example, for an inpatient hospital stay, the classification system is the diagnosis related group (DRG). Medicare uses separate payment systems for reimbursement to acute inpatient hospitals, home health agencies, hospice, hospital outpatient, inpatient psychiatric facilities, inpatient rehabilitation facilities, long-term care hospitals, and skilled nursing facilities.

For acute inpatient hospitals, the inpatient prospective payment system (IPPS) is used. Under the IPPS, each case is categorized into a diagnosis-related group (DRG). Each DRG has a payment weight assigned to it, based on the average resources used to treat Medicare patients in that DRG.

Other Medicare Prospective Payment Systems include:

Home Health Agencies

- The Home Health Resource Group (HHRG) is the PPS
- The assessment tool used to determine the HHRG is OASIS
- A predetermined base payment for each 60-day episode of care is based on the HHRG
- Payment is adjusted under certain conditions

Inpatient Rehabilitation Facilities

- The Case Mix Group (CMG) is the PPS
- The patient is assessed using the Inpatient Rehabilitation Facilities Patient Assessment Instrument (IRF-PAI)
- IRF-PAI classifies patients into groups based on clinical characteristics and expected resource needs
- The Patient Assessment Instrument (PAI) determines the patient's CMG
- The CMG determines the payment rate per stay

Skilled Nursing Facilities

- The Resource Utilization Group (RUG) is the PPS
- The patient is assessed using the Minimum Data Set (MDS) assessment tool
- Based on the MDS, the patient is placed into a RUG
- The RUG determines the facility's reimbursement rate

Outpatient Hospital

- The Ambulatory Payment Classification System (APC) is the PPS
- Included in this payment category are hospital-based clinics, ER, observation, and ambulatory surgery

- It is an encounter-based classification system
- Payment rates are based on categories of services similar in cost and resource utilization

Value-Based Purchasing

The Affordable Care Act established the Hospital Value-Based Purchasing (VBP) Program. VBP is a Centers for Medicare & Medicaid Services (CMS) initiative that rewards acute care hospitals with incentive payments for the quality of care they provide to Medicare beneficiaries. CMS bases hospital performance on an approved set of measures and dimensions grouped into specific quality domains. These domains vary depending on the program's fiscal year. For example, during the fiscal year 2016, the VBP Program used four domains that reflected hospital quality: the clinical process of care domain, the patient experience of care domain, the outcome domain, and the efficiency domain. VBP uses quality measures that hospitals already report to Medicare via the Hospital Inpatient Quality Reporting program.

Coding Methodologies

Medical coding is the transformation of healthcare diagnoses, procedures, and medical services into universal medical alphanumeric codes. The codes are used by healthcare providers, government health programs, health insurance companies, and others. Uses include:

- Reimbursement (filing and processing claims)
- Tracking infectious diseases (such as the flu, TB, and whooping cough)
- Tracking health conditions (such as diabetes, cardiovascular disease, and cancer)

International Classification of Diseases (ICD)

The International Classification of Diseases (ICD) coding system assigns a number or alphanumeric to describe diseases, traumas, and environmental circumstances leading to bodily harm. It is used to report medical diagnoses and procedures on claims as well as to gain data for public health surveillance. The code set, which was updated to ICD-10 in 2015, consists of two parts:

- ICD-10-CM – The diagnosis classification system for use in all United States healthcare treatment settings
- ICD-10-PCS – The procedure classification system used in the United States for inpatient hospital settings only

The ICD code is the diagnosis/reason for the encounter with the health system (e.g., chest pain, pre-op evaluation, diabetes).

Current Procedural Terminology (CPT)

Current Procedural Terminology (CPT) codes are maintained and copyrighted by the American Medical Association (AMA). They are a standardized form of identifying services provided, including medical, surgical, radiology, laboratory, anesthesiology, and evaluation and management services. Providers use CPT codes to report services performed to payers for reimbursement purposes, assigning a code for each procedure done during that visit. While the ICD-10 code tells the reason for the visit (e.g., chest pain), the CPT code lists the procedures performed (e.g., evaluation and management, venipuncture, ECG).

Diagnosis Related Group (DRG)

Medicare uses the Diagnosis Related Group (DRG) system as a basis of payment for hospital inpatient services. In an attempt to control costs, hospitals are paid based on the DRG for the admission rather than for each procedure performed or inpatient day.

DRG combines ICD-10 codes with patient demographics, discharge status, and the presence of complications or comorbidities to classify a hospital admission into a payment category, based on the assumption that similar diagnoses should have similar hospital resource use and length of stay patterns.

The ICD-10 is used in determining the DRG, and the DRG is used to determine reimbursement for Medicare and some other payers.

Diagnostic and Statistical Manual of Mental Disorders (DSM)

The Diagnostic and Statistical Manual of Mental Disorders (DSM) is the official classification and listing of mental disorders. Each diagnosis includes a diagnostic code that providers, institutions, and agencies use for billing and data collection. The newest in the series, the DSM-5, includes both the older ICD-9 code related to the disorder, as well as the updated ICD-10 code in parentheses. There may be multiple disorders associated with a given ICD code; for this reason it is recommended that the disorder be entered in the medical record by name as well as the code.

Models of Care

Accountable Care Organization

One of the principal ways the Affordable Care Act aims to reduce healthcare costs is by encouraging doctors, hospitals, and other healthcare providers to form networks, known as accountable care organizations (ACOs), that coordinate patient care. By increasing care coordination, unnecessary medical care can be reduced, and health outcomes can be improved.

Providers in ACOs are held jointly accountable for delivering care more efficiently by achieving measured quality improvements and reductions in the rate of spending growth. They become eligible for bonuses when this is accomplished. This may sound similar to an HMO, but unlike HMOs, patients are free to select which medical services they receive and from whom.

Core components of the ACO model of care are:

- Provider-led, with a strong base in primary care
- All providers, across the full continuum of care, are accountable for quality and cost related to a population of patients
- Payments are linked to quality improvements that reduce overall costs
- Performance is measured

Medicare ACO

The Affordable Care Act authorized the Center for Medicare and Medicaid Services (CMS) to create the Medicare Shared Savings program, which allows for the establishment of ACO contracts with Medicare.

A Medicare ACO is formed by a group of doctors, hospitals, and other healthcare providers who come together voluntarily to give coordinated, high quality care to the Medicare Fee-for-Service beneficiaries they serve. The goal of an ACO is to deliver seamless, high quality care for Medicare beneficiaries, in contrast to the fragmented care that has so often been characteristic of fee-for-service healthcare. By providing coordinated care, patients get the right care at the right time, while avoiding unnecessary duplication of services and preventing medical errors. The ACO is a patient-centered organization, where the patient and providers are partners in care decisions.

When an ACO succeeds in the dual goals of delivering high-quality care and spending healthcare dollars more wisely, it shares in the savings it achieves for the Medicare program. This incentivizes the ACO to improve the coordination and quality of care for all its patients.

To evaluate the healthcare quality performance of an ACO, CMS has established ACO Quality Measures. At the time of publication, there were 33 quality measures in the following four quality domains:

- Patient/Caregiver Experience
- Care Coordination/Patient Safety

- Preventive Health
- At-Risk Population

A complete list of the ACO Quality Measure can be found at: https://www.cms.gov/Medicare/Medicare-Fee-for-Service-Payment/sharedsavingsprogram/Downloads/ACO-Shared-Savings-Program-Quality-Measures.pdf

Patient Centered Medical Home (PCMH)

The Patient-Centered Medical Home provides comprehensive primary care for children, youth, and adults. This healthcare setting facilitates long-term partnerships between patients, their personal physicians, and when appropriate, patients' families. Healthcare workers advocate for their patients and provide the education and support patients need to participate in and make decisions for their own care. The goal is to attain optimal, patient-centered outcomes that respect patients' wants, needs, and preferences. Unlike the ACO, the PCMH is a single practice.

Principles of the Patient-Centered Medical Home

- Personal physician – Each patient has an ongoing relationship with a personal physician trained to provide first contact, continuous, and comprehensive care. This personal physician coordinates all care for the patient.
- Physician-directed medical practice – The personal physician leads a team of practicing healthcare providers who are collectively responsible for the ongoing care of the patient.
- Whole person orientation – The personal physician is responsible for providing for the patient's entire healthcare needs or appropriately arranging care with other qualified professionals. This includes care for all stages of life, acute care, chronic care, preventive services, and end of life care.
- Care is coordinated and/or integrated across all elements of the complex healthcare system (e.g., subspecialty care, hospitals, home health agencies, nursing homes) and the patient's community (e.g., family, public

and private community-based services). Care is facilitated by registries, information technology, health information exchange, and other means. This ensures that patients get required care when and where they need and want it, in a culturally and linguistically appropriate manner.

• Enhanced access to care is available through systems such as open scheduling, expanded hours, and new options for communication between patients, their personal physicians, and practice staff.

• Evidence-based medicine and clinical decision-support tools guide decision-making.

• Physicians accept accountability for continuous quality improvement through voluntary engagement in performance measurement and improvement.

• The patient's participation in decision-making and feedback is sought to ensure his or her expectations are being met.

• Information technology is utilized appropriately to support optimal patient care, performance measurement, patient education, and enhanced communication.

Health Home

Healthcare for individuals with multiple chronic conditions represent our nation's most costly and complex healthcare. According to the National Comorbidity Survey, of individuals with a mental illness 68% also have a physical health condition such as cardiovascular disease, diabetes, or hypertension. These high-need individuals often receive uncoordinated care that results in higher costs and poorer health outcomes.

People with mental illnesses and substance use disorders typically receive most of their care in community behavioral healthcare settings. Many are unable or unwilling to receive care in a primary care setting. Even when they do, coordination between behavioral health and medical services may be poor. For those individuals who have relationships with behavioral health organizations, care may be best delivered by bringing primary care, prevention services, and wellness activities onsite at behavioral health settings. This method is known as integrated healthcare.

Healthcare reform legislation established health homes as a new state Medicaid option for service delivery specifically for enrollees with chronic conditions. A Medicaid health home, as defined in Section 2703 of the Affordable Care Act, offers coordinated care to individuals with multiple chronic health conditions, including mental health and substance use disorders. The health home recognizes the importance of caring for the whole person.

The health home is a team-based clinical approach that includes the consumer, his or her providers, and family members, when appropriate. The health home builds linkages to community supports and resources, as well as enhances coordination and integration of primary and behavioral healthcare to better meet the needs of people with multiple chronic illnesses. The model aims to improve healthcare quality while also reducing costs. Health home services include: comprehensive care management; care coordination and health promotion; comprehensive transitional care from inpatient to other settings; individual family support; referral to community and social support services; and the use of health information technology to link services.

Health home services are available to adults and children who receive benefits from Medicaid and who have at least two chronic conditions, such as asthma, diabetes, heart disease, obesity, a mental health condition, or substance abuse disorder; one chronic condition and are at risk for another; or one serious and persistent mental health condition.

Federal health home guidance lays out service requirements emerging from the ACA. The required services (also termed "provider standards" in the guidance) include:

- Each patient must have a comprehensive care plan
- Services must be quality-driven, cost effective, culturally appropriate, person- and family-centered, and evidence-based

- Services must include prevention and health promotion, healthcare, mental health and substance use, and long-term care services, as well as linkages to community supports and resources

- Service delivery must involve continuing care strategies, including care management, care coordination, and transitional care from the hospital to the community

- Health home providers do not need to provide all the required services themselves, but must ensure the full array of services is available and coordinated

- Providers must be able to use health information technology (HIT) to facilitate the health home's work and establish quality improvement efforts to ensure that the work is effective at the individual and population level

What is the difference between a medical home and a health home?

	Medical Homes	**Health Homes**
Population Served	Serve all populations	Serve individuals with approved chronic conditions
Providers	Typically defined as physician-led primary care practices, but also mid-level practitioners and health centers	May include primary care practices, community mental health centers, federally qualified health centers, health home agencies, etc.
Payer(s)	Multiple payers (e.g., Medicare, Medicaid, commercial insurance)	Medicaid only
Care Focus	Focus on the delivery of traditional medical care (referral and lab tracking, guideline adherence, electronic prescribing, provider-patient communication)	Strong focus on whole health (including substance abuse, mental health, and primary care), social support, and other services (such as nutrition, home health, and coordinating activities)
Use of IT	For traditional care delivery	For coordination across continuum of care, including in-home (e.g., wireless monitoring)

Special Needs Plans (SNPs)

Medicare Special Needs Plans (SNPs) are a type of Medicare Advantage Plan (like an HMO or PPO) available to some participants with Medicare Parts A and B. Medicare SNPs limit membership to people with specific diseases or characteristics, and tailor their benefits, provider choices, and drug formularies to best meet the specific needs of the groups they serve. Medicare SNPs are approved by Medicare and run by private companies. Members receive all of their medical healthcare, hospital care, and prescription drug coverage through the plan.

According to Medicare guidelines, the SNP must limit membership to these three groups:

- People who live in certain institutions (such as a nursing home) or who require nursing care at home, or
- People who are eligible for both Medicare and Medicaid, or
- People who have one or more of these severe or disabling chronic conditions:
    - Chronic alcohol and other drug dependence
    - Autoimmune disorders
    - Cancer (excluding pre-cancer conditions)
    - Cardiovascular disorders
    - Chronic heart failure
    - Dementia
    - Diabetes mellitus
    - End-stage liver disease
    - End-stage renal disease requiring any mode of dialysis
    - Severe hematologic disorders
    - HIV/AIDS
    - Chronic lung disorders

- Chronic and disabling mental health conditions
- Neurologic disorders
- Stroke

Plans may also put further limits on membership at their own discretion. For example, a Medicare SNP may be designed to serve only people diagnosed with congestive heart failure. The plan might include access to a network of providers who specialize in treating congestive heart failure, and it would feature clinical case management programs designed to serve the special needs of people with this condition. The plan's drug formulary would be designed to cover the drugs usually used to treat congestive heart failure. People who join this plan would get benefits specially tailored to their condition and have all their care coordinated through the Medicare SNP.

Chronic Care Model

The Chronic Care Model is a method of caring for people with chronic disease in the primary care setting. It encourages practical, supportive, and evidence-based chronic disease management using a proactive (rather than responsive) approach. This approach results in patients who take an active part in their care. The Chronic Care Model has led to improved patient care and better outcomes for patients with chronic illness.

Six Components to the Chronic Care Model

1. Health System – This component addresses the culture, leadership, and practices of the organization, which encourages optimal management of chronic disease.

2. Delivery System – The delivery system provides efficient clinical care and self-management support. Rather than reactively treating the patient in crisis, the focus is on keeping the patient healthy and out of crisis by providing follow-up care after the patient leaves the doctor's office. For more complex patients, case management is provided.

3. Self Management Support – This component focuses on empowering patients to manage their healthcare. Providers and patients use a collaborative approach to identify problems, set priorities and goals, create treatment plans, and solve problems.

4. Decision Support – Treatment is determined by discussing evidence-based guidelines with the patient so he or she becomes a participant in the decision-making process. Providers must keep up to date on the latest evidences and involve specialists when appropriate.

5. Clinical Information Systems – This component focuses on the organization of patient data to ensure efficient and successful management of chronic disease.

6. Community Resources – Resources available in the community for care, peer support, and education expand on the health system's treatment of chronic illness.

Healthcare Delivery Systems

A healthcare delivery system is a combination of organizations and individuals that work together to provide healthcare to a population. They can be public or private sector, including for-profit and not-for-profit. Examples include managed care, the military medical care system, and integrated delivery systems.

Managed Care

Managed care organizations include HMOs and PPOs and provide healthcare to members using contracted providers. These providers may include physicians, hospitals, nursing homes, medical equipment suppliers, and diagnostic clinics. They agree to provide care at a discounted rate to members. See Managed Care Cost Containment under Cost Containment Principles for more information on Managed Care.

Integrated Delivery System

An integrated delivery system is a variety of providers and/or organizations that come together to provide a coordinated continuum of services to a defined population. It could join physicians groups and hospitals, as is the case with a Physician Hospital Organization, or an insurance company with hospital and physicians groups. If the integrated delivery system includes an insurance company, the physicians and hospitals are owned by or partners with the insurance company, rather than contracted by the insurance company (as with managed care organizations). The goal is to coordinate the seamless delivery of healthcare services.

Cost Containment Principles

Traditional Insurance Cost Containment

With traditional insurance, cost containment comes in the form of coinsurance, copayments, and deductibles.

A copayment is a set amount the patient pays each time a specific service is rendered. For example, a plan may require a $20 copayment for each doctor office visit, or a $15 copayment for a prescription refill. Each time a patient goes to the doctor or has a prescription refilled, he will be charged the copayment amount, regardless of whether his deductible has been met.

The deductible and coinsurance work together. The deductible is a specific amount of money the patient must pay for covered expenses before the insurance company begins paying. Once the deductible has been paid, the coinsurance kicks in, with the insurance company and the patient sharing the remaining costs.

To illustrate: A patient received a procedure costing $5,000, and his plan required a $500 deductible and 80%/20% copayment. The patient is first responsible for the $500 deductible. After that, the insurance company pays 80% of the remaining $4,500 (equaling $3,600), and the patient pays 20% (equaling $900). The patient is responsible for $1,400 in total: the $500 deductible and the $900 copayment.

Managed Care Cost Containment

In managed care, medical services are coordinated by the insurance company to decrease healthcare costs. The two main types of managed care organizations are Preferred Provider Organizations (PPOs) and Health Maintenance Organizations (HMOs).

The PPO contains costs by negotiating discounts for services with providers as a condition for being included in the PPO. By receiving a discount from providers, the PPO is able to reduce health insurance premiums and healthcare expenditures. In turn, patients' costs are covered by the insurance company at a higher percentage when they choose providers in the PPO. Patients may choose providers not included in the PPO but will pay more out-of-pocket.

HMOs provide healthcare services to members for a set yearly fee per member. Providing too much or too costly care could cause them to lose money. Preventive care is encouraged under this insurance structure, to avoid more costly corrective care. HMOs often use a Primary Care Provider (PCP) to act as a gatekeeper. The gatekeeper's role is to provide medical and preventative care and to coordinate patient care outside of his or her scope of practice.

Medicare and DRG Cost Containment

Medicare implemented the diagnosis related group (DRG) system, in which the DRG pays a fixed amount for a given diagnosis, rather than paying all costs related to an individual patient's treatment during his or her hospital stay. This predetermined amount is paid regardless of the actual cost of treating the patient. This approach provides a significant incentive for hospitals to decrease costs.

Managed Care Concepts

Managed care is a system of healthcare delivery whose goal is to maintain quality, cost-efficient care by managing the use, access, cost, quality, and effectiveness of services. Managed care organizations link the patient to the provider and/or service and include several types, such as a preferred provider organization (PPO), exclusive provider organization (EPO), point-of-service (POS) plan, and health maintenance organization (HMO).

PPO

PPOs contract with providers to deliver care at a discounted rate. The providers with whom they contract are considered "network providers." If the patient uses a provider who is not part of the network, he or she will incur greater financial responsibility for the healthcare services received.

EPO

An EPO is similar to a PPO in that a network of providers have agreed to provide care for the members at a discounted rate. In an EPO, however, a patient is not reimbursed for services if he chooses to receive healthcare outside the network.

Point-of-Service (POS)

The Point-of-Service Plan is a combination of PPO and HMO. The patient can choose to receive care in-network at little or no cost, or to go out of the network and incur larger out-of-pocket expenses.

HMO

HMOs reimburse providers by capitation, paying a fixed amount per-member-per-month for contracted services. Providers are not reimbursed for the specific services provided. If the member uses the services once, or more often, the provider receives the same payment. Services that are not included in the contract between the provider and the HMO can be "carve out" services. They are handled by other providers without penalty to the primary care physician (PCP). This is usually done for specialty services, such as transplant or mental/behavioral health.

HMOs often use the primary care physician as a "gatekeeper." A patient receives all primary and preventative care from the PCP, and any care needed that falls outside the PCP's scope of practice is referred out and coordinated by the PCP. Any care (other than emergency care) not coordinated through the PCP is not covered by the HMO.

There are four types of HMOs:
- Group Model HMO
- Network Model HMO
- Individual Practice Association (IPA) Model HMO
- Staff Model HMO

In the Group Model HMO, the HMO contracts with a multi-specialty physician group, where the physicians are employed by the group, not the HMO. The HMO and the group share profits or losses.

The Network Model HMO is similar to the group model but involves more than one group of physicians. In this model the HMO contracts with multiple groups of physicians and other providers to form a network of care.

The Individual Practice Association Model HMO contracts with physicians who provide healthcare to the HMO members for a negotiated rate. The physicians own their individual or group practices.

In the Staff Model HMO physicians are employed by the HMO and provide services exclusively to members of the HMO.

Utilization Management Principles and Guidelines

Utilization management ensures that services provided are medically necessary and provided at the appropriate and least costly level of care. Many organizations use Milliman Care Guidelines (MCG) or InterQual to assist in utilization management.

See Factors Used to Identify Acuity or Severity Levels for more information on MCG and InterQual.

The Utilization Review Process

1. Verify eligibility; that is, check that the patient is covered under the health plan, and that this coverage is primary. For example: The patient may have both Medicare and insurance through his employer. The preauthorization request would go through the primary insurance first.

2. Verify that the requested service is a covered benefit under the insurance contract. If it is a covered benefit, determine if it requires preauthorization. For example, bariatric surgery may be a contract exclusion. If it is a covered benefit, it may require preauthorization.

3. Gather clinical information to determine if the criteria are met for this service.

4. Review clinical information to determine if it meets criteria for medical necessity and level of care, documenting as per policy.

5. If guidelines are met, notify the requesting provider of the approval.

6. If guidelines are not met, it is sent for physician review. The physician will approve or deny it based on medical judgment, and the requesting provider is notified of the decision.

7. If it is denied, the patient or treating physician may appeal.

8. The medical director collects more information and reviews the case again. He or she may also speak with the treating physician or send the information to an independent third party physician with expertise in the specialty area of the request.

There are three main types of utilization management: prospective, concurrent, and retrospective.

Prospective reviews, or precertifications, are done prior to the elective admission or procedure to ensure the requested service is necessary, meets criteria for coverage, and is at the appropriate level of care.

Concurrent reviews include continued stay reviews and are conducted as the care is occurring. This includes reviews for admissions that were not precertified, as well as to extend care that was precertified. Concurrent reviews are done to ensure the client is receiving the correct care in a timely and cost effective manner.

The retrospective review is done after care has already occurred. This can occur when precertification was required but not obtained, such as in an emergency situation.

Factors Used to Identify Acuity or Severity Levels

The diagnosis is only one factor in evaluating the acuity level of the patient. Other factors that may be taken into account include:

- Comorbid conditions
- Intensity of intervention needed
- Complex medical needs
- Family/social support
- Polypharmacy
- Psychological/cognitive status

- Complex treatment plans
- Number of providers involved

Acuity or severity levels are used for staffing as well as ensuring that the client is receiving the correct level of service. Two tools used to ensure the client is receiving the correct level of service are Milliman Care Guidelines (MCG) and InterQual.

MCG provides evidence-based care guidelines spanning the continuum of care, including:

- Ambulatory care
- Inpatient and surgical care
- General recovery guidelines
- Recovery facility care
- Home care
- Behavioral health guidelines

InterQual Level of Care Criteria help healthcare organizations assess the clinical appropriateness of patient services across the continuum of care. The severity of illness, comorbidities, and complications, as well as the intensity of services being delivered, guide them to the most efficient, safest level of care.

InterQual Level of Care Criteria are available for:

- Acute care
- Acute pediatric
- Acute rehabilitation
- Long term acute care
- Subacute care and skilled nursing facility
- Home care
- Outpatient rehabilitation and chiropractic

Levels of Care and Care Settings

Acute Care

Acute care is the most intensive level of care, during which a patient is treated for a brief but severe episode of illness, for conditions that are the result of disease or trauma, and/or during recovery from surgery. Acute care is generally provided in a hospital by a physician and a variety of clinical personnel.

Long Term Acute Care Hospitals and Long-Term Care Hospitals

According to Centers for Medicare & Medicaid Services (CMS), long term acute care hospitals (LTAC)—also referred to as long term care hospitals (LTCH) and transitional hospitals—focus on patients who stay more than 25 days on average. Many of the patients in LTACs are transferred in from an intensive or critical care unit. LTACs specialize in treating patients who have one or more serious conditions but who may improve with time and care. Services provided in LTACs typically include comprehensive rehabilitation, respiratory therapy, head trauma treatment, and pain management.

Subacute Care/Transitional Care

Subacute care is for patients who are stable and do not require hospital acute care, but who require more intensive skilled nursing care, therapy, and physician services than are provided to the majority of patients in a skilled nursing facility. These services may include TPN, IV therapy, wound care, and other therapies such as speech therapy, physical therapy, occupational therapy, and respiratory therapy.

Inpatient Rehabilitation

Inpatient rehabilitation hospitals provide intense, multidisciplinary therapy to patients with a functional loss. To qualify for this level of care, patients must be able to tolerate a minimum of 3 hours of therapy per day, 5 to 7 days per week, and be medically stable.

Skilled Nursing Facility (SNF)

SNFs offer 24-hour skilled nursing and personal care (e.g., bathing, eating, toileting). They also provide rehabilitation services, such as physical therapy, occupational therapy, and speech therapy. Patients must be medically stable to qualify for SNF level of care. They also must need care from a skilled, licensed professional, such as a nurse or therapist, on a daily basis. Examples are complex wound care and rehabilitation when a patient cannot tolerate three hours of therapy per day.

Intermediate Care

Intermediate care is a level of care for patients who require more assistance than custodial care, and may require nursing supervision, but do not have a true skilled need. Most insurance companies do not cover intermediate care.

Home Health Care

Home health care provides intermittent skilled care to patients in their home. Services such as skilled nursing, physical therapy, occupational therapy, speech therapy, and medical social worker visits are provided by home health agencies. For a patient to qualify for home health care under Medicare, he must be deemed homebound. To qualify as homebound, the patient must be unable to leave his home or require great effort to leave.

Hospice Care

Hospice provides end of life care to patients with a terminal illness. It also supports their families. To qualify for hospice care, a physician must document that the patient's life expectancy is limited if the disease follows its normal course of progression. Hospice care can be provided in any setting, including the patient's home, in the hospital, in a skilled nursing facility, or in a freestanding hospice facility.

Custodial Care

Custodial care assists with personal and home care, such as ADLs (activities of daily living) and IADLs (instrumental activities of daily living). This level does not require the services of a skilled or licensed provider. Custodial care can take place in the home, a skilled nursing facility, or an assisted living facility, among other places. Medical insurance does not cover this level of care.

Alternative Care Facilities

Assisted Living

Assisted living facilities provide housing and support with ADLs and IADLs to residents. Services provided often include:

- Meals
- Medication reminders
- Transportation
- Housekeeping
- Laundry
- 24-hour staff
- Personal assistance with ADLs

Assisted living facilities do not provide medical care or skilled nursing care. The cost of assisted living is not covered by medical insurance; it is paid either by the individual and his or her family or, if purchased, a long-term care insurance policy. Medicaid waiver programs may also cover assisted living. States, not the federal government, regulate these types of facilities.

Group Homes

Residents of group homes are typically children or adults with chronic disabilities requiring continual assistance to complete ADLs/IADLs, or behavioral problems that make them dangerous to themselves or others. Group homes usually house fewer than eight residents who share common areas such as the kitchen, living room, and laundry facilities and are staffed by trained personnel. The residents, depending on their ability, do chores.

Residential Treatment Facilities

Residential treatment facilities house and provide therapy for patients with drug and alcohol addictions, emotional or behavioral problems, and/or mental illness. They are clinically focused and offer treatments such as psychoanalytic therapy, behavioral management, group counseling, family therapy, and medication management. Residents have usually been unsuccessful with outpatient treatments, but are not appropriate for an inpatient psychiatric unit.

Additional Resources

Adherence

Strategies to Enhance Patient Adherence: Making it Simple: http://www.ncbi.nlm.nih.gov/pmc/articles/PMC1681370/

PhRMA Improving Medication Adherence Issue Brief.pdf: http://phrma.org/sites/default/files/pdf/PhRMA_Improving%20Medication%20Adherence_Issue%20Brief.pdf

Hospice, Palliative, and End of Life Care

https://www.medicare.gov/Pubs/pdf/02154.pdf

https://www.medicare.gov/Pubs/pdf/11361.pdf

CMA / Hospice: http://www.medicareadvocacy.org/medicare-info/medicare-hospice-%20benefit/#HOW%20MUCH%20HOSPICE%20CARE%20WILL%20MEDICARE%20COVER

The Medicare Hospice Benefit.pdf: http://www.nhpco.org/sites/default/files/public/communications/Outreach/The_Medicare_Hospice_Benefit.pdf

Hospice-overview booklet: https://www.cms.gov/Medicare-Medicaid-Coordination/Fraud-Prevention/Medicaid-Integrity-Education/Downloads/hospice-overviewbooklet.pdf

Hospice Benefits - Medicaid.gov: https://www.medicaid.gov/medicaid-chip-program-information/by-topics/benefits/hospice-benefits.html

Home Health Care

Home health services I Medicare.gov: https://www.medicare.gov/coverage/home-health-services.html

Military Benefits Program

CHAMPVA: http://www.va.gov/purchasedcare/programs/dependents/champva/

Health Plans - TRICARE For Life I TRICARE: http://www.tricare.mil/tfl

TRICARE: http://www.tricare.mil/

Accountable Care Organization

Medicare: https://www.medicare.gov/Pubs/pdf/11588.pdf

Quality Measures and Performance Standards - Centers for Medicare & Medicaid Services: https://www.cms.gov/Medicare/Medicare-Fee-for-Service-Payment/sharedsavingsprogram/Quality_Measures_Standards.html

ACO summary factsheet pdf: https://www.cms.gov/medicare/medicare-fee-for-service-payment/sharedsavingsprogram/downloads/aco_summary_factsheet_icn907404.pdf

ACO-Shared-Savings-Program-Quality-Measures.pdf: https://www.cms.gov/Medicare/Medicare-Fee-for-Service-Payment/sharedsavingsprogram/Downloads/ACO-Shared-Savings-Program-Quality-Measures.pdf

Patient Centered Medical Home

Defining the Medical Home / Patient-Centered Primary Care Collaborative: https://www.pcpcc.org/about/medical-home

Health Home

Health Homes / Medicaid: https://www.medicaid.gov/medicaid-chip-program-information/by-topics/long-term-services-and-supports/integrating-care/health-homes/health-homes.html

Health Homes / SAMHSA-HRSA: http://www.integration.samhsa.gov/integrated-care-models/health-homes

Special Needs Plans

Special Needs Plans (SNP): https://www.medicare.gov/sign-up-change-plans/medicare-health-plans/medicare-advantage-plans/special-needs-plans.html

Special Needs Plans FAQ: https://www.medicare.gov/sign-up-change-plans/medicare-health-plans/medicare-advantage-plans/special-needs-plans-faq.html#collapse-3323

ICD-10

ICD-10 Overview: https://www.cms.gov/Medicare/Coding/ICD10/downloads/ICD-10Overview.pdf

Public Benefits Programs

Original Medicare (Part A and B) Eligibility and Enrollment - Centers for Medicare & Medicaid Services: https://www.cms.gov/medicare/eligibility-and-enrollment/origmedicarepartabeligenrol/index.html

What's Medicare?: https://www.medicare.gov/sign-up-change-plans/decide-how-to-get-medicare/whats-medicare/what-is-medicare.html

Compassionate Allowances Complete List of Conditions: https://www.ssa.gov/compassionateallowances/conditions.htm

SSA Fact Sheet: https://www.ssa.gov/sf/FactSheets/aianssavsssifinalrev.pdf

Medicare and Medicaid: https://www.cms.gov/

Medicare: https://www.medicare.gov

COBRA

FAQs about COBRA Continuation Health Coverage: https://www.dol.gov/ebsa/faqs/faq-consumer-cobra.HTML

Prospective Payment System

Prospective Payment Systems - General Information - Centers for Medicare & Medicaid Services: https://www.cms.gov/medicare/medicare-fee-for-service-payment/prospmedicarefeesvcpmtgen/index.html

Financial Resources

Reverse Mortgages - Long-Term Care Information: http://longtermcare.gov/costs-how-to-pay/paying-privately/reverse-mortgages/

Home & Community-Based Waivers: https://www.medicaid.gov/medicaid-chip-program-information/by-topics/waivers/home-and-community-based-1915-c-waivers.html

Financial Planning-Special Needs Trusts: http://www.americanbar.org/newsletter/publications/law_trends_news_practice_area_e_newsletter_home/0501_estate_financialplanning.html

What Is a Special Needs Trust? / SpecialNeedsAnswers: http://specialneedsanswers.com/what-is-a-special-needs-trust-13601

Pooled Special Needs Trusts: https://www.nolo.com/legal-encyclopedia/pooled-special-needs-trusts.html

Patient Health Questionnaire

PHQ: http://www.integration.samhsa.gov/images/res/PHQ%20-%20Questions.pdf

Case Management Process

Case Management Knowledge I CCMC's Case Management Body of Knowledge (CMBOK): http://www.cmbodyofknowledge.com/content/case-management-knowledge-2

Chapter Two:
Psychosocial Concepts
and Support Systems

An effective case manager must understand everything that impacts the client and his ability to reach an optimal level of functioning. This includes, but is not limited to, support systems, psychosocial aspects, family dynamics, financial factors, culture, spirituality, and religion.

Interpersonal Communication

Interpersonal communication is the process of exchanging ideas, thoughts, and feelings between individuals. Case managers must be skilled at communicating effectively with patients, family members, caregivers, providers, and team members. Interpersonal communication involves conveying information effectively but also requires active listening.

Active listening is a fundamental part of interpersonal communication. To listen effectively, avoid jumping to conclusions or making premature judgments. Active listening can be demonstrated by nodding the head, making eye contact, repeating what is said, or note-taking. Note-taking should be kept to a minimum, however, so as not to spend more time looking at the computer or notepad than at the person speaking. Ask open-ended questions whenever possible, as they provide more information, are considered less threatening, and develop trust.

There are four components to communication:

- Sender
- Message
- Receiver
- Context (e.g., values, health beliefs, cultural background, pain, etc.)

Barriers to effective communication include:

- Physical interference (e.g., background noise, a non-private setting)
- Psychological noise (e.g., pain, hunger, anger, anxiety)
- Barriers to processing information (e.g., information overload, educational deficit, cognitive deficit)
- Perceptual barriers (that is, prejudices of the listener formed by his or her unique experiences, cultural background, and value system)
- Structural barriers (that is, layers of bureaucracy or other difficulty in reaching the other person)

In addition to verbal and written communication, there is nonverbal communication. The case manager should be aware of the nonverbal communication she is both giving and receiving. For example, a client who avoids eye contact or looks away when answering questions may not be telling the truth. On the other hand, the case manager should be sure her own nonverbal communication is showing that she is actively listening to the client.

Build trust and rapport in communicating with clients by finding common ground, such as shared goals. Build trust over time by doing what you say you will do, when you say you will do it.

Communication with or within a group is more complex than communication with an individual due to group dynamics. Group dynamics are the way members of a group relate to each other and the way the group relates to those outside the group. Group dynamics include:

Roles – The roles and identities that develop within the group, such as leader, authority, participant, follower.

Norms – The acceptable standards of behavior within the group that are shared by group members.

Conformity – Adjusting one's behavior to align with the norms of the group.

Interview Techniques

The client interview is a purposeful conversation and a collaborative effort between the case manager and the client. The client interview is the primary manner for obtaining information about the client to create an effective care plan, so it is imperative that the information obtained be complete and accurate. Therefore, the case manager should have good interview skills. The following steps can be taken to facilitate a successful interview.

Preparation

The interview should be scheduled for a time when there are no anticipated interruptions for either the client or the case manager. When scheduling the interview, the case manager should let the client know approximately how much time to allow and what information will be required. For example: "Mr. Smith, we will take approximately 30 minutes and need a list of your current medications and physicians' names."

Prior to the interview, review available information from the client's chart, medical records, prior encounters, etc. The reviewed materials are not a substitute for the client interview.

Prevent interruptions or distractions by silencing cell phones, turning off the TV, closing the door, or any other appropriate action. If the interview is over the telephone, make sure the client is at a location where he or she will be comfortable talking about private health information. For example, if he or she is talking on a cell phone at the grocery store, arrange a time when the client will have privacy.

Introduction

The case manager should introduce herself, including her title and whom she is employed by. For example, an insurance case manager should reveal to the client that she works for the insurance company. The case manager should then explain her role and inform the patient of the purpose of the interview. The case manager should ask the patient how he would like to be addressed. It is also a good idea to inform the client why the case manager will be asking so many questions.

Establish Rapport

The case manager should create an environment that helps the client feel safe disclosing sensitive, personal information. He or she will feel more comfortable disclosing personal information, health history, problems, and concerns after positive rapport has been established. Do so by showing an authentic interest in the client as a human being. Ask the client a question about his or her job, family, or interests.

Assessment

The case manager should start the interview asking open-ended questions, giving the client the opportunity to tell his story. When the patient is speaking, the case manager should actively listen. Guided questions can be used to get more specific information or to redirect the interview.

Summary

The case manager can close the interview by providing a summary of information obtained and explaining the plan of care. The client and case manager should collaborate on goals.

Motivational Interview

The motivational interview is a collaborative, client-centered approach to interviewing that focuses on helping the client discover his or her motivation for change. This is done through identification, examination, and resolution of the ambivalence to change.

Principles of motivational interviewing include:
- Express empathy – See things as the client sees them
- Support self-efficacy – Focus on the client's skills, strengths, and previous successes
- Roll with resistance – Do not increase resistance by confronting the client when resistance occurs
- Recognize discrepancy – Help the client see the discrepancy between where he is and where he wants to be, without judgment

Motivational interviews avoid confrontation and instead focus on collaboration and partnership between the client and the case manager, building trust. The case manager and client do not have to agree on everything; they may respectfully maintain differing opinions. But rather than impose her ideas on the client, the case manager should draw ideas out of the client. Lasting change is more likely when the client discovers his or her own reasons, motivation, and skills to change. Ultimately it is up to the client to follow through with these changes.

The basic approach used in motivational interviewing can be remembered by the acronym OARS:

Open-ended questions – Help the client explore reasons and strategies for change

Affirmations – Build rapport and help the client see himself in a positive way

Reflections – Guide the client toward resolving ambivalence by focusing on the positive and negative aspects of changing or not changing

Summaries – Show interest and understanding, while calling attention to important points in discussion

Health Coaching

Health coaching is secondary prevention, meaning that the client already suffers from a chronic disease. The goal of health coaching is to lessen the impact of the disease. Health coaching uses a coordinated and proactive approach to managing care for patients with chronic illness. Health coaches, or disease managers, take on a different role than traditional medical professionals. Rather than instruct patients on what they should do, health coaches assist patients to achieve their healthcare goals. The role of the health coach is to support, encourage, and empower patients to achieve their goals using evidence-based guidelines. Outcomes measured in health coaching include: decreased

Emergency Department visits and hospitalizations, adherence to guidelines, and/ or clinical measures such as maintaining blood pressure or Hemoglobin A1c level. Successful disease management results in a higher quality of life, lower healthcare costs, and clinical improvement for the client.

The main reason patients do not change health behaviors is ambivalence, because they:

- Are not ready
- Do not think they are able to change
- Do not have a plan
- Do not have support

The Health Coaching Process

Establish a relationship – The case manager develops positive rapport with the patient to foster trust.

Motivational interview – The case manager helps the patient discover which issues are most concerning. The case manager then engages the client to elicit "change talk" and to discover inner motivations to make the necessary changes. Change talk can be fostered by asking questions such as, "How does your condition interfere with things you like to do?" The goal is to increase the patient's awareness of the potential problems, consequences, and risks related to his or her unhealthy behavior, as well as to discover what motivates the patient.

Goal setting – The case manager assists the patient in setting goals and helps the patient discover options for achieving the goals. The case manager continues to monitor the patient's progress and focuses on successes toward the goals.

Behavioral Change Theories and Stages

For greater success in helping a client make positive changes, a case manager or health coach should determine where the client is in the 5 Stages of Change.

5 Stages of Change

1. Pre-contemplation

2. Contemplation

3. Preparation

4. Action

5. Maintenance

In the pre-contemplation stage, the individual does not intend to take action in the foreseeable future. He may not think about the change or he may be resistant to it. Pressuring the client at this stage is usually not effective. *"I don't want to quit smoking."*

In the contemplation stage, the individual considers a change in the next six months but has not committed to it. He may be open to information on the benefits of change and how to successfully do so. *"I know I need to quit smoking, I just don't know how."*

Preparation is when the individual actively plans to make a change within the next month. They may even have taken small steps toward change. *"I got my nicotine patches today and have set my quit date."*

Action is the stage when the individual has successfully made a change and has sustained it for less than six months. He will be seeking reinforcement and encouragement. *"I have not had a cigarette in nine days."*

When the change has been sustained for more than six months, maintenance has been achieved. Relapse can occur at any level, however.

Client Engagement

Improved client engagement has been shown to result in better health outcomes, better quality of care, and improved patient safety. Client engagement has such an impact on health outcomes that the Affordable Care Act has identified it as an integral component of quality in accountable care organizations (ACOs) and patient centered medical homes. Client engagement involves the exchange of information between the client and provider, as well as the client taking an active role in care decisions.

Factors that can impact client engagement include:

- Motivation
- Attitudes
- Beliefs
- Knowledge
- Cognitive ability
- Education
- Health literacy
- Past experiences with the health system
- Degree of self-efficacy
- Trust between patient and provider

Client engagement involves the case manager building a therapeutic relationship with the client to gain his trust and maximize his involvement. The engaged client will be taking action, such as exercising regularly, taking medications as prescribed, or monitoring blood sugars.

When the client is engaged, the case manager is working with him, not merely talking to him. When a client is not engaged, it can seem as though the case manager is swimming against the current.

To engage the client, the case manager must understand what is important to him. What are his concerns, values, beliefs, and goals? It is easier to engage the client with this information in hand. The motivational interview can be used to obtain this knowledge.

See more information on the motivational interview under Interview Techniques.

Client Activation

Client activation describes the knowledge, skills, ability, willingness, and confidence a person has that allows him to become actively engaged in managing his own health and healthcare. It is very specific to the client.

The terms *client activation* and *client engagement* are often confused or used interchangeably. Although they are similar, they are not the same. Client engagement builds on client activation with behaviors such as maintaining a healthy diet, exercising regularly, or obtaining preventative care.

Example: An activated client has the knowledge, skills, resources, and confidence to manage his diabetes. The engaged client monitors his blood sugars, maintains his diet, and exercises daily.

The Patient Activation Measure (PAM) was developed by Judith Hubbard of the University of Oregon to measure a client's activation level. Studies have shown that clients with higher PAM scores are better able to engage in their health and have better health outcomes and lower healthcare costs.

Clients with lower PAM scores are more likely to feel overwhelmed with managing their health. They are also less likely to understand and have confidence in their role in their own healthcare. By understanding a client's level of activation, healthcare clinicians can create individualized care plans to increase activation and engagement.

Ways to increase activation include:
- Meeting clients where they are
- Personalizing care
- Educating
- Empowering
- Increasing confidence
- Breaking down actions into small, manageable steps

Client Empowerment

The Case Management Society of America (CMSA) lists empowering the client as one of the roles and functions that case managers perform. A case manager empowers her client, as well as his family, caregivers, and members of the healthcare delivery team, by supporting and educating them so they can understand and access quality, efficient healthcare.

By providing education on treatment options, community resources, insurance benefits, psychosocial concerns, and the role of the case manager, the client, caregiver, and healthcare delivery team can better problem solve and explore options of care to achieve the desired outcomes. The empowered client is able to manage his care and practice self-advocacy, increasing adherence to the plan of care.

Client Self-care Management

Self-management in patients with chronic disease refers to their behaviors and the decisions they make that affect their health. Self-management support is the care and encouragement provided to people with chronic conditions (and their families) to help them manage their health on a daily basis, make informed decisions about care, engage in healthy behaviors, and direct their care. It involves collaboration between the client and case manager to foster ownership by the client.

Shared decision-making between the provider and patient requires the patient to be informed. Informed decision-making requires two-way communication between the patient and provider, wherein the patient's unique situation, beliefs, and priorities are discussed alongside the treatment options, so the patient can make the best treatment choice. It supports the ethical principle that patients have the right to decide what care is appropriate for them, including the right to accept or decline healthcare.

Case managers empower patients to be informed and active decision-makers in their healthcare. They encourage patients to practice self-advocacy by explaining treatment options and providing education on the disease or injury, community resources, and insurance coverage. The case manager never makes a decision for the client, but rather guides the client in decision-making.

Health Literacy Assessment

Health literacy is not simply the ability to read. Health literacy is the ability to obtain, communicate, process, and understand basic health information. It requires a complex set of reading, listening, analytical, and decision-making skills, as well as the ability to apply these skills to health situations. In addition to basic literacy skills, health literacy requires knowledge of health topics, such as how the body works and causes of disease. This is the foundation needed to understand treatment options and consent documents. Health literacy also requires numeracy skills such as calculating insulin dosage, measuring medication, understanding nutrition labels, and interpreting lab results. Even successful and well-educated people may have low health literacy.

The National Assessment of Adult Literacy measures the health literacy of adults living in the United States using four basic performance levels: Proficient,

Intermediate, Basic, and Below Basic. Only 12% of the population was found to have a proficient health literacy level. This means that nearly 9 out of 10 adults in the United States are not proficient in understanding health-related information.

Knowing this can help case managers ask their clients better questions. Instead of asking, "Do you understand your discharge instructions?," it is more appropriate to ask specific questions about how they are taking their medications, when they are following up with their doctor, and which signs and symptoms to report. Case managers should also use common language, not medical terms, when speaking with patients.

Low health literacy has been linked to higher rates of hospitalization and Emergency Department usage, less frequent use of preventive services, and a greater likelihood of taking medicines incorrectly. People with limited health literacy are also more likely to have chronic conditions and are less able to manage them effectively. All of these outcomes are associated with higher healthcare costs.

Those at highest risk for low health literacy are:

- Older adults
- Racial and ethnic minorities
- Those having less than a high school degree or GED
- Individuals whose income is at or below poverty level
- Non-native speakers of English

Signs of low health literacy include deferring questions about their health history to a family member, stating that a family member handles their medications, frequent hospitalizations or emergency room visits, misuse of medications, and not being able to verbalize the plan of care.

The case manager can use single question assessments to assess health literacy, such as:

- How often do you have someone help you read hospital materials?

- How confident are you filling out medical forms by yourself?
- How often do you need to have someone help you when you read instructions, pamphlets, or other written material from your doctor or pharmacy?

There are also formal health literacy instruments. The most widely used are:

Rapid Estimate of Adult Literacy in Medicine (REALM) – Assesses the ability of adult patients to read common medical words and lay terms for illnesses and body parts. The examiner scores the patient on the number of words pronounced correctly, but no attempt is made to determine if the patient actually understands the meaning of the word. This assessment is only available in English.

The Newest Vital Sign – A tool that tests literacy skills for both numbers and words. It is available in English and Spanish. It is designed to assess a patient's health literacy skills quickly and simply, taking only three minutes to administer. The patient is given a specially designed ice cream nutrition label to review and is asked a series of questions about it. Based on the number of correct answers, healthcare providers assess the patient's health literacy level.

Test of Functional Health Literacy Assessment (TOFHLA) – A more complex assessment that takes 20 minutes or more to administer and consists of two parts, each with different types of questions.

The first part consists of 17 multiple choice questions that test a patient's ability to interpret numbers and documents. The second part assesses reading comprehension by asking patients to read 3 passages of text, in which a blank line replaces key words. The patient chooses the word that makes most sense from a word bank. A shorter version of the test is available and is known as the S-TOFHLA. It can be completed in about 12 minutes and contains 4 multiple choice question and 2 reading passages. Both the TOFHLA and the S-TOFHLA are available in English and Spanish.

Wellness and Illness Prevention Programs, Concepts and Strategies

Maintaining wellness and prevention of disease can improve the length and quality of a patient's life. It can also be cost-effective. The case manager should assess the client for risk factors including diet and activity level, tobacco and alcohol use, as well as compliance with immunizations and screenings. Education should be provided when needed.

Many employers offer wellness programs through which participants are screened for risk factors and offered free education and support in areas where improvement is needed. Some of the more popular programs include smoking cessation, weight loss, and stress control.

Vaccines

Case managers may assess for updated vaccines, including the yearly flu vaccine, the pneumococcal vaccine, and shingles vaccine. Patients with chronic conditions are particularly vulnerable to the flu and pneumonia.

Diet

Case managers should assess the patient's diet and access to proper nutrition. When a deficit is identified, the case manager can provide nutritional education and refer the patient to community resources.

Physical Activity

Engaging in regular physical activity is one of the most important factors in maintaining and improving health. Physical activity strengthens bones, increases muscle, reduces depression and stress, and helps maintain a healthy weight. Thirty minutes of moderate physical activity a day is recommended. Case managers can provide education and referrals to community resources to help clients find an activity that meets their needs.

Mammograms

The American Cancer Society recommends women age 40 and older have yearly mammograms.

Colorectal Cancer Screening

Men and women of average risk should begin screening for colorectal cancer at the age of 50.

Psychological and Neuropsychological Assessment

During the initial exam and on subsequent interactions with the client, case managers should assess:

- Temporary or permanent functional changes
- Physiological, psychological, or social problems
- Problems functioning in the community

If the need for further assessment is indicated, a referral for neuropsychological testing should be made. A medical evaluation should be performed prior to the psychological evaluation to rule out underlying medical conditions that can cause behavioral symptoms.

A neuropsychological evaluation should be performed on clients who have suffered a head injury to determine if there are any deficits. Neuropsychological testing is done by a neuropsychologist and includes a review of medical records, a personal interview, a review of psychiatric records, and psychological testing. Information is collected regarding the client's cognitive, behavioral, motor, linguistic, and executive functioning. If areas of deficits are found, a program can be created to address these areas.

Other Psychological, Neuropsychological, Functional, and Assessment Tools

Rancho Los Amigos Levels of Cognitive Functioning

The Rancho Los Amigos Scale of Cognitive Functioning is used to follow the recovery of the traumatic brain injury (TBI) patient. The scale is divided into eight stages, from coma to appropriate behavior and cognitive functioning. Those stages include:

I - Unresponsive to all stimuli

II - Generalized response to stimuli

III - Localized response to stimuli

IV - Confused/agitated

V - Confused/inappropriate, non-agitated behavior

VI - Confused/appropriate behavior

VII - Automatic/appropriate behavior

VIII - Purposeful/appropriate behavior

DSM-IV

Psychiatric diagnoses are categorized by the *Diagnostic and Statistical Manual of Mental Disorders, 4th Edition*, known as the DSM-IV. The DSM uses a multi-axial approach to diagnosis because it is rare that a person's mental health is not affected by other factors in his or her life. The DSM assesses five dimensions as described below.

Axis I: Clinical Disorders

Clinical disorders are what we typically think of as the diagnosis, such as depression, schizophrenia, or social phobia. These disorders may come and go.

Axis II: Developmental Disorders and Personality Disorders

These are lifelong and enduring disorders. Developmental disorders include autism and intellectual disability, disorders which are typically first evident in childhood. Personality disorders are clinical syndromes that have more long-lasting symptoms and impact the individual's way of interacting with the world. They include paranoid, antisocial, and borderline personality disorders.

Axis III: General Medical Conditions

These are physical conditions that play a role in the development, continuance, or exacerbation of Axis I and II Disorders.

Axis IV: Psychosocial and Environmental Problems

Events in a person's life, such as poverty, dysfunctional family, death of a loved one, unemployment, or starting a new job or college, that might have some impact on the person's ability to function and can impact the disorders listed in Axis I and II.

Axis V: Global Assessment of Functioning Scale

The clinician rates the person's level of functioning both at the present time and the highest level within the previous year. This helps the clinician understand how the first four axes are affecting the person and what changes could be expected.

The rating scale provides scores from 10 to 100, with low scores signaling persistent danger of severely hurting oneself or others, and high scores indicating superior functioning in a wide range of activities.

Glasgow Coma Scale (GCS)

Measures level of coma in the acute phase of injury.

The Mini-Cog Test

A brief (approximately 3-minute) assessment instrument used to screen for cognitive impairment, Alzheimer's, and related dementia. The Mini-Cog involves two parts, a 3-item recall and a Clock Drawing Test (CDT) given in 3 steps.

Step 1: The person being tested is given the name of 3 common objects and is asked to repeat them back.

Step 2: They are asked to draw a clock showing a specified time. This serves as a recall distractor and a screening tool.

Step 3: The person is asked to name the 3 objects from Step 1.

The Mini-Mental Status Exam

An assessment of cognitive function consisting of 11 questions covering:

• Orientation

• Registration (immediate memory)

• Attention and calculation

• Recall

• Language and praxis

The test takes approximately 10 minutes to administer and can be used to help diagnose cognitive impairment following a head injury or the presence of dementia. It is also used to assess the severity and progression of the impairment. Scores of 25-30 are considered normal, and scores <24 are abnormal, with decreasing scores indicating increasing severity of impairment.

Hamilton-D

Used by healthcare professionals to measure the level of depression of a client.

Minnesota Multiphasic Personality Inventory (MMPI)

The MMPI is a psychological test that assesses personality traits and psychopathology. It is most commonly used by mental health professionals to assess and diagnose mental illness. It can only be given and interpreted by a psychologist trained to do so.

Psychosocial Aspects of Chronic Illness and Disability

How an individual is affected by chronic illness and disability may be influenced by numerous factors, including:

- Age
- Gender
- Race
- Culture
- Extent of functional limitation
- Prognosis
- Coping styles
- Past experiences
- Social support
- Family support
- Socioeconomic status

The effects of chronic illness and disability are individual and involve:

- Social and family relationships
- Economic well-being
- Activities of daily living
- Social activities
- Work activities
- Grief
- Distortion of body image

A disability is considered chronic when the impaired function will never be completely eliminated. The case manager should assess not only the physical effects of chronic illness or disability, but also the psychosocial effects on both the patient and his family and caregivers. A chronic disability changes the client's self-perception and role. Case managers must understand the patient's role in the family (such as breadwinner or caregiver) and how that role is affected by the illness or disability. This will help the case manager understand the impact of the illness or disability. The case manager can then design a plan of care to educate, support, and counsel the patient to manage symptoms, carry out treatments, and make lifestyle and behavior changes.

Self-efficacy

Self-efficacy is one's belief in his or her own ability to succeed, and it plays a major role in the client's outcome. The more self-efficacy a client possesses, the more likely he or she will persevere when obstacles arise. For a behavioral change to take hold, the client must know what to do, believe it is beneficial, and believe it is attainable.

Factors that influence self-efficacy include the client's physiological and psychological state, mastery of experiences, vicarious experiences, and social persuasion. With each experience the client masters, he finds evidence that he has the ability to succeed. Witnessing others in similar situations overcome their obstacles is further proof that perseverance can lead to success. Continuous positive persuasion strengthens personal beliefs regarding success.

The case manager can foster and encourage self-efficacy in the client in many ways. She can provide affirmation, motivation, and encouragement. She can facilitate goal setting that will promote mastery by helping the client create small, attainable goals. Many disabled individuals have made major contributions to society. The case manager can tell these individuals' stories to remind the client what is possible. She can also assist the client reach optimal physical and psychological function by making referrals as needed.

Family Dynamics

When a family member becomes ill or injured there are numerous implications for the family financially, emotionally, physically, and socially. The client's family is usually his source of support, and when necessary, his caregiver. Families provide the majority of long-term care for patients. To best serve the patient, case managers need to provide support and advocacy for the family as well as the patient.

To best assess the situation, the case manager needs to understand the client's role in the family. Was he the breadwinner? Was he the caregiver to another family member? How does his illness affect his role? No matter the client's role in the family, the illness or injury will disrupt the family norms. An extended or severe illness will require modifications of family responsibilities.

Case managers also need to understand the family's dynamics. Many families have issues that can affect their ability to adapt to a crisis situation such as an illness or injury. Are family members dealing with alcoholism, mental illness, depression, abuse, or their own health issues? Is this an intact family or a divorced family with stepparents, stepchildren, and/or stepsiblings? Issues that existed before will be intensified during times of stress.

An adaptive family is able to adjust to crisis; this is important to helping the patient reach his goals. An adaptive family possesses the ability to:
- Be flexible
- Problem solve
- Communicate effectively
- Seek and accept help

A maladaptive family is unable to meet the changing needs of the family. Maladaptive families:
- Overindulge the patient
- Foster patient dependency

- Abandon other family members
- Abandon the patient
- Deny the patient's condition
- Rely on a single person to provide all assistance to the patient
- Fail to seek assistance or ask for help

The case manager's ability to understand the family dynamics will assist her in providing interventions and resources as needed. She can make a referral to family counseling or support groups. She can also encourage the family to maintain as much of their normal routine as possible, to take care of themselves, and to ask for help.

Assessing for caregiver support and family coping is an ongoing process. Everyone may come together initially and set aside family issues, but maladaptive family dynamics may surface later. The primary caregiver may become burned out as initial support may diminish over time.

Support Programs

Initial and ongoing assessments should be conducted to identify additional support needs. If needs are identified, the case manager can refer the patient to one of the many local and national disease-based programs to provide education, financial resources, and peer support. The American Cancer Society, for example, offers patients assistance with lodging when traveling for care away from home, local transportation to and from treatments and appointments, and online support groups, along with many other resources.

Support programs are also available for caregivers. Many communities have local support groups, and national organizations, such as the Alzheimer's Foundation of America, offers support services and strategies for caregivers.

For patients with deeply held spiritual beliefs (identified during the spiritual assessment upon enrollment in case management), pastoral counseling may be an integral part of their treatment.

Bereavement counseling can aid in the loss of a loved one, as well as other losses brought on by illness or tragedy. Local hospice agencies are a good resource for bereavement counseling and will provide this service to anyone, not just their clients.

Resources for the Uninsured or Underinsured

Like the uninsured, the underinsured may have difficulty obtaining healthcare. For example, if an individual has medical insurance but no prescription coverage, he can see the doctor and get a diagnosis and prescription to treat the problem, but he may not be able to afford to fill the prescription. A client suffering a stroke may exhaust a 30-visit limit for outpatient rehabilitation long before reaching his maximum potential.

Even with the best insurance coverage, some services are not covered, such as home modifications, caregivers, healthy meals, and transportation to doctor appointments. Case managers often need to remove barriers to care by referring clients to available resources beyond their health benefit, such as community resources. Community resources are also available for caregivers, providing support and respite.

Fraternal and religious organizations often offer a variety of resources ranging from building wheelchair ramps to food pantries. The Area Agency on Aging assists clients 60 and older and those with disabilities to live in their homes and communities for as long as possible by providing services in the five categories below.

Information and access services:

- Health insurance counseling
- Information and referral assistance
- Transportation
- Caregiver support
- Retirement planning education

Community-based services:

- Employment services
- Adult day care
- Senior centers
- Group meals

In-home services:

- Meals on wheels
- Homemakers
- Telephone reassurances
- Energy assistance and weatherization
- Home health services
- Respite care
- Personal care services

Housing:

- Senior housing
- Alternative community-based living facilities

Elder rights:
- Legal assistance
- Elder abuse prevention programs
- Ombudsman services

Meal delivery can help an elderly person maintain independence and continue living at home. The Meals On Wheels Association of America is a national network of more than 5,000 Senior Nutrition Programs that operate in all 50 states delivering nutritious meals to seniors.

People with limited income may have to choose between food and their medications. Nearly all communities have local food banks to provide nutritious food for needy members of the community. In addition, many drugstores and grocery stores chains have programs that allow patients to refill their generic medications for free or a nominal fee. Some pharmaceutical companies offer pharmacy assistance programs, through which some of their medications can be obtained by uninsured or low-income individuals at a discount or no cost. Many states also have pharmacy assistance programs for seniors and other qualifying individuals.

Other community resources include:
- Disease organizations (American Cancer Society, MS Society, National Kidney Fund, Alzheimer's Association)
- Charity organizations (United Way)
- Service organizations (Rotary, Elks, Lions Club)
- Make-A-Wish
- American Association of Retired Persons (AARP)
- Public Health Departments

In addition to the resources above, government programs, such as the Katie Beckett Waiver and the Children's Health Insurance Program (CHIP), may help. The Katie Beckett Waiver enables severely disabled children and adults to be cared for at home and to be eligible for Medicaid based on the affected individual's income and assets alone. Without the waiver, the income of legally liable relatives is counted when the individual is cared for at home. The Children's Health Insurance Program (CHIP) provides health coverage to children in families with incomes too high to qualify for Medicaid, but who do not have, and can't afford, private health insurance coverage. Other programs are available and vary from state to state.

Behavioral Health Concepts

Dual Diagnoses

Dual diagnosis describes patients with coexisting mental illness and substance abuse disorders. The mental illness must meet criteria for diagnosis by the *Diagnostic and Statistical Manual of Mental Disorders* (DSM-IV). Dual diagnoses are not uncommon, with about half of those with a severe mental illness and one-third of those with mental illness also struggling with substance abuse. The prognosis for patients with mental illness who abuse drugs and/or alcohol is worse than for patients who do not.

Psychiatric treatment is more successful with patients who are not actively abusing these substances. For this reason, the first step is often for the patient to stop using— or, if the patient is addicted, to detox the patient. Additional treatment may include individual counseling, support groups, and medications to help the patient develop coping skills, build self-confidence, and manage the symptoms of mental illness.

Patients with dual diagnoses are often a challenge for case managers. They are less likely to follow through with their treatment plan by missing appointments and failing to take medications. The case manager will find greater success if he or she can help the patient find the motivation to comply with the treatment plan.

Substance Use, Abuse, and Addiction

Substance use includes alcohol, over the counter drugs, prescription drugs, and illegal drugs. Substance use does not equal substance abuse.

The American Psychiatric Association's *Diagnostic and Statistical Manual of Mental Disorders, 4th Edition* (DSM-IV) defines substance abuse as a maladaptive pattern of substance use leading to clinically significant impairment or distress, as manifested by one (or more) of the following, occurring within a 12-month period:

- Recurrent substance use resulting in a failure to fulfill major role obligations at work, school, or home (e.g., repeated absences or poor work performance related to substance use; suspensions or expulsions from school; neglect of children or household)

- Recurrent substance use in situations in which it is physically hazardous (e.g., driving an automobile when impaired by substance use)

- Recurrent substance-related legal problems (e.g., arrests for substance-related disorderly conduct)

- Continued substance use despite having persistent or recurrent social or interpersonal problems caused or exacerbated by the effects of the substance (e.g., arguments with spouse about consequences of intoxication; physical fights)

The case manager must assess for substance abuse or addiction since it may complicate the diagnosis and/or treatment of medical conditions. Most patients will not readily admit that they have an addiction problem. The CAGE tool is available for screening substance abuse. It consists of four questions:

1. "Have you ever felt you should **C**ut down on drinking/drug use?"

2. "Have people **A**nnoyed you by criticizing your drinking/drug use?"

3. "Have you ever felt **G**uilty about your drinking/drug use?"

4. "Have you ever taken a drink/used drugs in the morning to steady your nerves or get rid of a hangover (**E**ye opener)?"

Answering yes to two of the questions provides strong indication for substance abuse. Answering yes to three of the questions confirms the likelihood of substance abuse or dependency.

Withdrawal from alcohol and drugs can cause anxiety, tachycardia, tremors, grand mal seizures, insomnia, nausea and/or vomiting, and hallucinations. Detoxification treats these physical effects.

The case manager's role is to support the treatment plan, provide encouragement to the patient and his family/caregivers, and refer to AA or similar organizations.

Levels of care for addiction are based on the program's structure, including the setting, intensity, and frequency of services.

Level I: Outpatient Treatment

Less than 9 hours per week of directed treatment and recovery services.

Level II: Intensive/Partial Hospitalization Treatment

Regularly scheduled sessions for a minimum of 9 hours per week in a structured program, with the opportunity for the client to interact in his own environment.

Level III: Medically Monitored Intensive Inpatient

Inpatient treatment with 24-hour observation, monitoring, and treatment by a multidisciplinary staff.

Level IV: Medically Managed Intensive Inpatient

Medical and nursing services along with the full resources of a hospital, available on a 24-hour basis.

Community-based programs such as Alcoholics Anonymous and Narcotics Anonymous have been found to be the most successful in treating substance abuse. Inpatient hospitalization for substance abuse is not usually the preferred method of treatment.

Crisis Intervention Strategies

A crisis can refer to any situation in which the client perceives the inability to effectively problem-solve and/or cope. A situation that is a crisis to one individual may not be a crisis to another. Not all crises involve danger, but if the patient is in danger, the first priority is his safety. Get professional help, even if the patient resists. Never leave him alone. If he is admitted to an inpatient facility, he will require 1:1 observation.

If at any time the patient is thought to be at risk for suicide, the case manager should ask directly if he has a plan to commit suicide. If there is any doubt about the patient's safety, he should be admitted. If safety is not an issue, help him develop good support systems or refer him to a support group, counselor, therapist, or psychiatrist as appropriate. Remove items such as weapons or large quantities of medications from the patient's access. Complete frequent follow-up assessments to evaluate the effectiveness of the interventions.

Suicide risk factors include:
- History of prior suicide attempt
- Family history of suicide
- Living alone
- Recently divorced or widowed
- History of mental illness
- Chronic illness
- History of substance abuse

- Unemployed
- Recent loss
- Hopelessness or helplessness
- Risk-taking behavior
- Giving away prized possessions
- Lack of interest in future plans

After safety is established, listen to the client to assess his state of need. Always allow him to tell his story and express his full emotions without the fear of being judged. Assist the client to assess available resources and strategies that have worked for him in the past. Collaborate on finding alternative coping mechanisms and setting goals, while focusing on the client's strengths.

Conflict Resolution Strategies

When faced with a conflict, it is important for all parties to focus on the goal, rather than the person or persons they are in conflict with. It is also important to keep communication open and to avoid bringing emotion and/or reactivity into the process. If the case manager believes emotion or reaction are taking over, it is best to call for a "cooling off period" where both parties can take a break, resuming when the focus can be placed back on the goal.

The following five conflict resolution strategies are listed from most to least desirable for most situations. Remember that the situation will dictate the best conflict resolution strategy to utilize.

1. Collaboration – This strategy meets the needs of all parties involved.

2. Negotiation – Finding a solution that gives everyone a partial win, with everyone giving something up. This strategy is most useful when there is a standstill in negotiations and the parties are approaching a deadline.

3. Accommodation – This meets the needs of the other party at the expense of one's own needs.

4. Competitive – This style takes a firm stand. It is useful in emergency situations when decisions need to be made fast. It can also be utilized when someone is trying to take advantage of a situation. When used inappropriately, however, this strategy can leave the other party feeling resentful, bullied, or unsatisfied.

5. Avoidance – This style avoids the conflict by allowing the default action.

Multicultural, Spiritual, and Religious Factors

Culture is comprised of languages, beliefs, values, traditions, and customs. The case manager is to practice cultural competence with awareness and respect for diversity. He or she should be aware of, and responsive to, cultural and demographic diversity of the population. Case managers are to take part in ongoing cultural competency training to enhance their work with multicultural populations.

A cultural assessment, including an assessment of the client's linguistic needs, should be included in the case manager's initial client assessment. While it is necessary for a case manager to understand general cultural norms as they relate to healthcare, it is more important that she understands that each patient is an individual with his own individual, family, and cultural beliefs. Sometimes these cultural beliefs conflict with the treatment plan. When this happens the case manager should attempt to adjust the treatment plan to work within the cultural limits. If this is not possible, the case manager must educate the client on the possible effects of not complying with the treatment plan. This should be done respectfully without coercing the client. Ultimately it is the client who chooses to follow the treatment plan.

At times, the client's cultural beliefs may be very different from the case manager's. This can influence how a case manager views her clients. The case manager must respect the client's beliefs, even though she may not agree with them. It can be helpful to acknowledge cultural differences with the client, and reassure the client that the case manager's job is to educate him and support his decisions.

Case managers should assess the client's linguistic needs and identify resources to enhance proper communication. This may include use of interpreters and material in different languages and formats. When using an interpreter it is best to use a professional interpreter—not a family member—whenever possible.

Spirituality as It Relates to Health Behavior

Spirituality is a broad concept with many perspectives. In general, it includes a sense of connection to something bigger than us, and it typically involves a search for meaning in life. For some people spirituality is synonymous with religion, but a person does not have to have a religious belief to be spiritual.

It is important to have an understanding of clients' spiritual and religious views, as the views often impact choices they make in regard to healthcare. For example, if a patient believes that he has no control over his destiny, he may feel that lifestyle changes or medical intervention will not change the inevitable, and therefore decline treatment or lifestyle changes. On the other hand, if the patient believes that life is precious and all means should be exhausted in prolonging it, he may be unwilling to accept the withdrawal of life-sustaining treatment, even when death is inevitable. It is also important to understand that some religious beliefs can affect healthcare choices; for example, Jehovah's Witnesses do not accept blood transfusions, and some Pentecostal Christians will refuse medical treatment due to their strong belief in miraculous healing.

Assessing a patient's spiritual needs is an important part of the initial assessment with the client. With this information the case manager can refer the patient to resources for spiritual counseling. During times of illness, patients often rely on their spiritual beliefs to cope. Spiritual practices tend to improve coping skills, provide optimism and hope, promote healthy behavior, decrease feelings of depression and anxiety, and encourage a sense of relaxation. By relieving stressful feelings and promoting healing ones, spirituality can positively influence immune, cardiovascular, hormonal, and nervous systems. Studies have shown that terminally ill patients with a higher spiritual well-being were less likely to have depression and thoughts of suicide.

Case managers should avoid judging a patient's healthcare decision based on spiritual beliefs. When possible the case manager can offer alternatives that are within the patient's beliefs.

End of Life Issues

Case managers can help clients and families make informed decisions regarding end of life care that can prevent or relieve suffering and make an impact on the costs that are often associated with end of life care. The case manager should understand the client's wishes regarding end of life care. Once these wishes are understood, the case manager can provide education as to the options available and how to ensure the client's wishes are acted on. This could be in the form of a palliative care consult, hospice, and/or advance directives such as a Durable Power of Attorney, Living Will, and/or Do Not Resuscitate.

Patient Self-Determination Act

The Patient Self-Determination Act (PSDA) amends titles XVIII (Medicare) and XIX (Medicaid) of the Social Security Act. It requires all hospitals, skilled nursing facilities, home health agencies, hospice programs, and health maintenance organizations that receive Medicare and Medicaid reimbursement to recognize the living will and durable power of attorney for healthcare. Under the PSDA they must:

- Ask patients if they have an advance directive
- Inform the patient of their rights under state law to make decisions concerning their medical care
- Not discriminate against persons who have executed an advance directive
- Ensure legally valid advance directives are implemented to the extent permitted by state law
- Provide education programs for staff, patients, and the community on ethical issues concerning patient self-determination and advance directives

Advance Directives

Advance directives come in two forms: those that dictate the kind of medical treatment to be given or withheld, such as a living will or do not resuscitate, and those that appoint an agent or proxy to make healthcare decisions. Both forms only go into effect if the person is unable to make the decision for himself. All states have their own advance directive forms and requirements. Next is a description of the different types of advance directives available. Note that the names may vary slightly from state to state.

Living Will

A living will states which specific medical treatments the designated person would like to receive or have withheld. These treatment can include, but are not limited to:

- Mechanical ventilation
- Dialysis
- Tube feedings
- IV fluids
- Antibiotics
- CPR

Health Care Power of Attorney

Also known as a Durable Power of Attorney, this type of advance directive stipulates who is to make healthcare decisions for the person named if he is unable to make decisions for himself.

Do Not Resuscitate

A do not resuscitate (DNR) is a request not to have CPR performed.

Hospice Care

Hospice provides comprehensive end of life care and support to terminally ill patients and their families. The care provided by hospice extends beyond the patient's death by providing bereavement support for the family. To qualify for hospice care, a physician must document that the patient's life expectancy is limited, usually six months or less, if the disease follows its normal course of progression.

Hospice care is a team approach, coordinated by a case manager. A hospice medical director, home health aide, social worker, and chaplain are all involved with the plan of care. Hospice care also covers medications related to the hospice diagnosis and durable medical equipment. Not covered under the hospice benefit is room and board and treatment to cure the disease.

Hospice care can be provided in an inpatient setting, such as a hospital or a freestanding hospice facility, or the patient's home. "Home" is wherever the patient lives and does not need to be a traditional home; it can be an assisted living facility, nursing home, homeless shelter, or any other place the patient calls home.

The hospice case manager's goals are unique to each patient but frequently include:

- Control pain and other symptoms, giving the patient a better quality of life
- Provide the patient and family information they need to make informed

decisions regarding treatment and the plan of care to ensure the patient has a dignified death

• Coordinate and facilitate care

A Do Not Resuscitate (DNR) is not necessary before enrolling in hospice, but patients and families are educated on this topic, with the goal of having the DNR in place before a patient's death.

Tools used to assess for hospice appropriateness:

Karnofsky Performance Scale – Measures performance status on a scale of 0-100%, with 0 being deceased and 100 being normal with no complications. A score of less than 70% (cares for self but is unable to carry on normal activities or work) can be one of the criteria for hospice.

Eastern Cooperative Oncology Group (ECOG) Performance status scale – A 0-4 scale with 0 being fully active and 4 completely disabled.

Palliative Performance Scale (PPS) – Uses five observer-rated domains (ambulation, activity level/evidence of disease, self-care, intake, and level of consciousness) correlated to the Karnofsky Performance Scale (0-100). It is a reliable tool that aids in determining appropriateness for hospice, especially for cancer patients.

Palliative Care and Symptom Management

Many people use the terms palliative care and hospice interchangeably, but there are important distinctions to make. Palliative care can be employed with a patient at any stage of a severe illness. It can be used concurrently with curative treatment. Palliative care is not dependent on prognosis. Alternatively, hospice care provides comprehensive care, including palliative care, for terminally ill patients with a life expectancy of six months or less, who are no longer receiving curative treatment.

Palliative care is specialized medical care for patients suffering from serious and chronic illnesses, such as cancer, CHF, COPD, kidney failure, and ALS, just to name a few. The goal of palliative care is for the patient and his or her family to maintain the best quality of life possible, by managing symptoms such as pain, fatigue, dyspnea, constipation, nausea, anorexia, and depression. Palliative care can be given alongside other medical treatment, such as chemotherapy and radiation, and can improve the ability to tolerate those treatments.

Palliative care is a team approach, with the core team including the doctor, nurse, and social worker. Other members may be brought into the team as needed, including a chaplain, pharmacist, dietitian, massage therapist, or music therapist, among others. The palliative care team works together with the patient's other doctors and providers to anticipate, prevent, and treat suffering. The majority of palliative care today is provided by hospice, although there are palliative care specialists and practices.

The main goal of palliative care is symptom management to allow the best quality of life for the patient. To achieve this, some medication dosages and routes of administration may be different from the standard. It is also not uncommon for medications to be used off label. For example, anticonvulsants may be used to treat pain, or morphine to ease dyspnea.

Also see the section on Hospice, Palliative, and End of Life Care in the chapter Care Delivery and Reimbursement Methods.

Abuse and Neglect

There are numerous types of abuse and neglect, including physical, emotional/ psychological, sexual, financial, and medical neglect. The elderly are at increased risk for abuse, with those over age 80 at the highest risk. The perpetrators of abuse and neglect are most often family members, with the majority of them being spouses and adult children. As case managers are often in contact with the caregivers, they should be aware of the risk factors of abusers. These risk factors include mental illness, alcohol and drug abuse, history of abuse, inability to cope with stress, depression, lack of support from other potential caregivers, and caregiver reluctance.

If the case manager identifies that the patient is at increased risk, she can try interventions that may reduce the threat of abuse.

- Ensure the caregiver receives proper training and education on his or her responsibilities
- Help the caregiver develop a support system and identify support groups and respite care
- Inquire about situations that frustrate or anger the caregiver and help him or her identify appropriate responses
- If necessary, assist with the arrangement for paid caregivers or placement of the patient in the appropriate long-term care setting

Nurses are mandated reporters of abuse or neglect. If abuse or neglect is suspected, they must notify Adult Protective Services. Depending on the case, the police may also be notified. The case manager should carefully document all communication and findings objectively.

General Signs and Symptoms of Abuse and Neglect

- Changes in personality or behavior
- Sudden change in physical or financial status
- Tension or arguments between caregiver and client
- Failure to take medications (or not refilling in appropriate time frame)
- Caregiver's refusal to allow elder to be seen alone

Types of Abuse and Neglect

Neglect – The failure or inability to provide for basic needs. This can be intentional or unintentional.

Emotional/Psychological Abuse – The infliction of anguish, pain, or distress through verbal or nonverbal acts, such as gestures or writing, resulting in trauma. This also includes threats of harm used to intimidate a person into complying or cooperating.

Examples of emotional and psychological abuse and neglect include:

- Verbal assaults
- Insults
- Threats
- Intimidation
- Humiliation or embarrassment
- Harassment
- Disregarding needs
- Damaging or destroying property
- Isolation
- Ridicule
- Coercion
- Mental cruelty
- Inappropriate sexual comments
- Controlling behavior (such as prohibiting or limiting access to transportation, telephone, money, or other resources)

Physical Abuse – The use of physical force, such as hitting, beating, pushing, shaking, slapping, kicking, burning, and pinching, that results in physical pain, bodily injury, or impairment. Also included in physical abuse is force-feeding and the use of drugs and physical restraints.

Signs of physical abuse and neglect include:

- Dehydration
- Poor hygiene and/or grooming
- Weight loss
- Unexplained bruises, burns, scars, broken bones, or sprains

- Restraint marks
- Skin breakdown
- Vaginal or rectal pain
- Abrasions, bleeding, or bruising in the genital area
- Lab results showing overdose of medication

Financial Abuse and Neglect – Failing to use the patient's income or assets for the benefit, support, and maintenance of the patient. The illegal, unauthorized, or improper use of the resources of the patient.

Examples of financial abuse and neglect include:

- Forgery
- Theft
- Coercion
- Deception
- Fraud

Additional Resources

Patient Engagement and Activation

Only Talk Patient Engagement When Activation Is Involved: http://www.huffingtonpost.com/stan-berkow/only-talk-patient-engagem_b_4913747.html

What The Evidence Shows About Patient Activation: Better Health Outcomes And Care Experiences; Fewer Data On Costs: http://content.healthaffairs.org/content/32/2/207.abstract

Development of the Patient Activation Measure (PAM): Conceptualizing and Measuring Activation in Patients and Consumers: http://www.ncbi.nlm.nih.gov/pmc/articles/PMC1361049/

Insignia Health: http://www.insigniahealth.com/products/pam-survey

Health Policy Briefs: https://www.healthaffairs.org/healthpolicybriefs/brief.php?brief_id=86

Health Literacy

Health Literacy - Fact Sheet: Health Literacy Basics: http://health.gov/communication/literacy/quickguide/factsbasic.htm

Health Literacy - National Network of Libraries of Medicine: https://nnlm.gov/outreach/consumer/hlthlit.html#Skills_Needed_for_Health_Literacy

Health Literacy - Fact Sheet: Health Literacy and Health Outcomes: http://health.gov/communication/literacy/quickguide/factsliteracy.htm

Health & Literacy Special Collection: http://healthliteracy.worlded.org/assess_individuals.htm

End of Life Issues

The Patient Self-Determination Act. A matter of life and death. - PubMed - NCBI: http://www.ncbi.nlm.nih.gov/pubmed/10141946

H.R.4449 - 101st Congress (1989-1990): Patient Self Determination Act of 1990 l Congress.gov l Library of Congress: https://www.congress.gov/bill/101st-congress/house-bill/4449

What are Advance Directives? - CaringInfo: http://www.caringinfo.org/i4a/pages/index.cfm?pageid=3285

State-by-State Advance Directive Forms l Everplans: https://www.everplans.com/articles/state-by-state-advance-directive-forms

Chapter Three:
Quality and Outcomes
Evaluations and Measurements

Everyone—from policymakers to payers to accrediting bodies—is requiring the healthcare industry to focus on quantifiable outcomes. With the recent trend of healthcare reimbursement being tied to quantifiable outcomes, there is heightened focus on quality, efficiency, safety, and value in healthcare.

Case managers are in a position to shine in this environment, by means of their opportunities to directly affect outcomes from patient admission through discharge and beyond. Case managers must be familiar with quality and outcome measures and must understand their role in ensuring organizations meet them.

Quality and Performance Improvement Concepts

Case management programs should maintain a quality management function to show the value case management brings to both the client and the healthcare organization. The case management program could be eliminated if it does not demonstrate the value it brings.

Case management programs should promote objective monitoring and evaluation of the case management services rendered. The program should also provide written documentation of the quality or performance improvement goals, as well as strategies to monitor and evaluate the case management quality. Data related to case management services and quality performance goals should be tracked, and steps should be taken to enhance areas identified as needing improvement.

Quality improvement is a systematic, data-driven effort to measure and improve client services and the quality of healthcare services provided. It is accomplished by monitoring, correcting, and preventing quality deficiencies and noncompliance with the standards of care. It is not intended to attribute blame, but rather to discover where errors are occurring and to develop systems to prevent errors.

Performance improvement focuses on the healthcare organization's functions and processes and how these affect the ability to reach desired outcomes and meet the client's needs. Both quality improvement and performance improvement can be prospective or retrospective and aim to improve how things are done.

There are several measurements for performance improvement, including:

1. Process

2. Structure

3. Outcomes

Measures of Process examine what is actually done in giving and receiving care and how well clinical guidelines are followed.

For example:

- Percentage of clients screened for colon cancer
- Percentage of patients with diabetes given regular foot care
- Percentage of children who are vaccinated
- Percentage of heart patients who receive beta blockers in the hospital

Measures of Structure assess the capacity of a healthcare organization to provide services to individual patients or a community, and for managed care organizations to ensure they have network providers in place to meet members' needs. For example:

- Accreditation status
- Staffing ratios
- Board-certified providers
- Access to specific technologies or units (e.g., MRI, burn unit)

Measures of Outcomes examine the health status of the patient as a result of healthcare. For example:

- Adherence rates
- Control of blood pressure
- Acceptable HgA1c levels
- Mortality

Hospital Consumer Assessment of Healthcare Providers and Systems (HCAHPS)

HCAHPS (pronounced "H-caps"), also known as the CAHPS Hospital Survey, is a nationally standardized survey of patients' perspectives of their hospital experience. The survey was developed by Centers for Medicare and Medicaid Services (CMS) in partnership with Agency for Healthcare Research and Quality (AHRQ) and endorsed by National Quality Forum (NQF).

The results of this survey allow for an objective comparison of hospitals on topics that are important to consumers. These survey results are publicly reported, creating increased transparency of healthcare, as well as incentives for hospitals to improve the quality of care they provide.

The Deficit Reduction Act of 2005 and the Affordable Care Act of 2010 impacted HCAHPS measurements. In accordance with the Deficit Reduction Act, hospitals subject to the Inpatient Prospective Payment System (IPPS) annual payment update provisions must collect and submit HCAHPS data in order to receive their full IPPS annual payment update. IPPS hospitals that fail to publicly report the required quality measures, which include the HCAHPS survey, may receive a reduced payment. The Affordable Care Act includes HCAHPS among the measures used to calculate value-based incentive payments in the Hospital Value-Based Purchasing program.

Quality Indicators Techniques and Applications

Quality indicators are defined as objective and quantitative measures of the structures, processes, or outcomes of care. Indicators provide a quantitative starting point for clinicians, organizations, and planners striving to achieve improvement in care and the processes by which patient care is provided. Indicators themselves do not provide definitive answers but they do suggest good quality care or potential problems.

The following are types of quality indicators and examples of what they measure.

Clinical – Pain management, level of function, rehospitalization, hospital-acquired conditions, avoiding hospitalization, rates of morbidity, mortality, and complications

Financial – Cost per case, cost per service, cost per day, length of stay

Productivity – Wait time for appointment, length of time client spends in transplant evaluation before being presented to the Medical Review Board, length of stay

Utilization – Cesarean section delivery rate, incidental appendectomy in the elderly, hysterectomy rate, appropriate level of care, appropriate level of service

Quality – Decubitus ulcer rate, foreign body left in during a procedure, hospital-acquired infection

Client experience – Satisfaction, comfort

Monitoring healthcare quality is impossible without the use of quality indicators. They create the basis for quality improvement and prioritization in the healthcare system by identifying potential quality concerns, identifying areas requiring further investigation, and tracking changes over time. Measuring and monitoring of quality indicators can serve many purposes, including:

- Documenting quality of care
- Comparing care over time
- Comparing care between places (e.g., geographical, hospital)
- Supporting accountability, such as accreditation and/or regulation
- Supporting quality improvement projects

The information needed to assess quality indicators can be acquired by systematic or non-systematic methods. Ideally, systematic methods should be based on scientific evidence, but this type of evidence is not available for many areas of healthcare. In these cases quality indicators can be based on a combination of evidence and the professional opinion and experience of clinicians.

One popular method for obtaining professional opinions for quality indicators is the Delphi technique, a structured process that uses a series of questionnaires, known as rounds, to gather information. Rounds are held until a group consensus is reached. A primary benefit of the Delphi technique is that a large number of professionals in various locations with diverse scopes of expertise can be included.

Non-systematic methods are quick and simple, but because they are not evidence-based, the resulting indicators may be less credible than those developed using systematic methods. Even so, indicators developed using non-systematic methods, such as case studies, can be useful. Because these methods are easier to perform than systematic methods, they allow for quicker application.

Quality indicators measure aspects of care, but measuring itself does not improve quality or outcomes. Measuring may identify a problem, so quality improvement can be applied.

Quality Improvement Techniques

In general, quality improvement methods use the Plan-Do-Study-Act (PDSA) approach. Two other popular quality improvement techniques used in healthcare are Six Sigma and Lean. The techniques are described below.

Plan-Do-Study-Act approach

In the PDSA approach, the Plan stage identifies a process that has yielded less than ideal outcomes. The Do stage measures key performance attributes. Study devises a new approach, and Act integrates the redesigned approach into the process.

Six Sigma approach

Six Sigma for healthcare uses a 5-step approach to process improvement, known by the acronym DMAIC: define, measure, analyze, improve, and control.

> Define – In the Define step, the goal and scope of the project is identified (e.g., decreasing hospital length of stay (LOS) after hip replacement).

Measure – Measure involves collecting available data for the process to develop a baseline. In this step the team also identifies all interrelated business processes to find areas of possible performance enhancement (e.g., determining current LOS for hip replacements, and listing all disciplines involved with the patient).

Analyze – The objective of the third step, Analyze, is to reveal the root cause of inefficiencies and to determine solutions to overcome these inefficiencies. Group discussions and analysis of the data collected in the Measure step will reveal where changes can provide the most effective results (e.g., Physical Therapy and Occupational Therapy are not available over the weekend, resulting in delay of treatment; availability of these disciplines over the weekend will eliminate this delay).

Improve – The fourth step, Improve, develops and implements methods to address the process deficiencies uncovered during analysis. By the end of this phase, a test run of the change is completed and feedback is analyzed (e.g., PT and OT are available on the weekend; LOS is reevaluated).

Control – In the Control stage, metrics are developed to assess the success of the implemented changes. If adjustments must be made, the cycle will continue. Alternatively, the new changes may be made permanent, and the project is complete.

Lean approach

The Lean approach to quality improvement emphasizes reducing waste to increase value. Focus is placed on the customers, including patients, payers, providers, and regulatory bodies, to determine what they consider valuable. Lean provides tools for analyzing process flow and delay times to distinguish "value-added" work from "non-value-added" work. When the non-value-added work (or "waste") is identified, it is eliminated. The elimination of waste can increase value, decrease costs, and create a better customer experience.

Accreditation Standards and Requirements

Accreditation is usually a voluntary process, provided by an external organization, in which trained peer reviewers evaluate a healthcare organization's compliance with nationally accepted standards, as well as the accrediting body's pre-established performance standards. Although accreditation is technically voluntary, it is often required to be eligible to receive reimbursement from Medicare, Medicaid, and many third party payers. Accreditation is also often required by local, state, or federal regulations.

Accreditation is regarded as one of the key benchmarks for measuring the quality of an organization. It identifies the organization as credible and reputable, dedicated to ongoing and continuous compliance with the highest standard of quality. There is consistent evidence that accreditation significantly improves the process of care provided by healthcare services and improves clinical outcomes.

Preparing for accreditation provides a healthcare organization the opportunity to improve the quality of care they provide to patients by establishing, reviewing, and revising standards, measuring performance, and providing education. It is a chance for the organization to identify its strengths and its opportunities for improvement.

An accrediting body might review the organizational structure, policies and procedures, quality outcomes, performance improvement, patients' rights, professional improvement, leadership, fiscal operations, and clinical records, as well as compliance with federal, state, and local laws.

There are numerous accrediting bodies covering the various healthcare industries, including but not limited to:

- URAC
- Joint Commission
- Commission on Accreditation of Rehabilitation Facilities (CARF)
- National Committee for Quality Assurance (NCQA)

- National Quality Forum (NQF)
- Agency for Healthcare Research and Quality (AHRQ)

They have their own standards and requirements for awarding accreditation based on their corner of the healthcare industry, but the objective is always to ensure consumer protection by requiring safe, quality care.

Sources of Quality Indicators

The next few pages are devoted to some of the accrediting bodies and sources of quality indicators case managers should be familiar with. A general overview is given for each, with examples when appropriate. For more information or a complete list of standards, a link is provided. It is recommended to look up any terminology that is not understood for more details.

CARF

The Commission on Accreditation of Rehabilitation Facilities (CARF) is an independent, non-profit accreditor of health and human services. CARF's standards focus on improved service outcomes, client satisfaction, and quality service delivery. Each set of standards is developed with the input of providers, consumers, payers, and other experts from around the world. Each year, CARF updates its standards to ensure they are relevant and guide excellent service.

CARF provides accreditation in the following areas:
- Medical rehabilitation
- Durable medical equipment, prosthetics, orthotics, and supplies
- Aging services
- Behavioral health, including opioid treatment programs

- Employment and community services
- Child and youth services
- Business and services management networks

Additional information can be found on CARF's website at http://www.carf.org/Accreditation/

URAC

URAC, formerly known as the Utilization Review Accreditation Commission, accredits over 20 types of healthcare organizations, including Accountable Care, Case Management, Community Pharmacy, Disease Management, and Health Plan. URAC accreditation standards and requirements vary based on the type of organization being accredited.

As a credentialing body for case management, URAC believes that effective case management puts the consumer at the center of all healthcare decisions, and that this is essential to ensuring consumers get the right care, in the right setting, at the right time. URAC's Case Management accreditation allows case management standards to be applied across all healthcare settings, such as medical and social case management, behavioral health providers, hospital case management, disability and workers' compensation case management, and emerging practices. URAC has 40 CORE standards in 14 areas that apply to case management organizations.

URAC's case management standards cover:

- Organizational structure
- Policies and procedures
- Regulatory compliance
- Departmental coordination
- Oversight of delegated functions
- Review of marketing and sales material

- Business relationships: written business agreements, client satisfaction
- Information management: business continuity, information confidentiality and security, confidentiality of individually identifiable health information
- Quality management: quality management program, resources, and requirements; quality management committee, documentation, projects, project requirements, and consumer organizations
- Staff qualifications
- Staff management: training programs, operational tools and support, assessment programs
- Clinical staff credentialing and oversight roles
- Healthcare system coordination
- Consumer protection and empowerment: consumer rights and responsibilities, safety mechanisms, satisfaction, and health literacy

Additional information can be found on URAC's website at https://www.urac.org/accreditation-and-measurement/accreditation-and-measurement/

NCQA

The National Committee for Quality Assurance (NCQA) provides accreditation for healthcare organizations and managed care organizations. They also sponsor, support, and maintain a collection of standardized performance measures known as the Health Plan Employer Data and Information Set (HEDIS). The information from HEDIS helps employers and other purchasers evaluate health plan operations.

The case management accreditation provided by the NCQA is based on comprehensive and evidence-based guidelines, and it is dedicated to quality improvement. The core of the accreditation program is care coordination, patient-centeredness, and quality of care. It can be used for case management programs in provider, payer, population health, or community-based organizations.

NCQA's Case Management Accreditation:

- Directly addresses how case management services are delivered, not just the organization's internal administrative processes

- Gets to the essence of care coordination and quality of care

- Is designed for a wide variety of organizations. It is appropriate for health plans, providers, population health management organizations, and community-based case management organizations

- Focuses on ensuring the organization has a process for safe transitions

The standards address how case management programs:

- Identify people in need of case management services

- Target the right services to clients and monitor their care and needs over time

- Develop personalized, patient-centered care plans

- Monitor clients to ensure care plan goals are reached and make adjustments as needed

- Manage communication among providers and share information effectively as people move between care settings, especially when they transition from institutional settings

- Build in consumer protections to ensure people have access to knowledgeable, well-qualified case management staff

- Keep personal health information safe and secure

NCQA standards also call for case management program staff to stay up to date on the latest evidence and case management techniques and work toward continuous improvement in patient outcomes and satisfaction. Additional information on NCQA's case management accreditation can be found at https://www.ncqa.org/Portals/0/Programs/Accreditation/case%20mgmt-5_8.2.12.pdf

NQF

The National Quality Forum (NQF) is a not-for-profit, nonpartisan, membership-based organization whose mission is to improve the quality of healthcare. NQF promotes consensus among a wide variety of stakeholders from both the public and private sector, around specific standards that can be used to measure and publicly report healthcare quality.

NQF has endorsed performance measures to quantify healthcare processes, outcomes, patient perceptions, and organizational structure or systems that provide high-quality care. Once a measure is endorsed by NQF, it can be used by hospitals, healthcare systems, and government agencies like the Centers for Medicare & Medicaid Services for public reporting and quality improvement.

NQF performance measures:
- Bring together working groups to foster quality improvement in both public and private sectors
- Endorse consensus standards for performance measurement
- Ensure that consistent, high-quality performance information is publicly available
- Seek real time feedback to ensure measures are meaningful and accurate

NQF-endorsed measures are evidence-based. Together with the delivery of care and payment reform, they help:
- Make patient care safer
- Improve maternity care
- Achieve better health outcomes
- Strengthen chronic care management
- Hold down healthcare costs

More information on NQF can be found at: http://www.qualityforum.org/Measures_Reports_Tools.aspx

CMS

Quality Improvement Organizations of the Centers for Medicare & Medicaid Services

The Centers for Medicare & Medicaid Services (CMS) is a federal agency within the U.S. Department of Health and Human Services. Quality Improvement Organizations (QIOs) work under the direction of CMS; they are a group of health quality experts, clinicians, and consumers, organized to improve the care delivered to people covered by Medicare. By law, the mission of the QIO Program is to improve the effectiveness, efficiency, economy, and quality of services delivered to Medicare beneficiaries. QIOs do this by analyzing data and patient records to identify areas for improvements in care. They also ensure patients' voices are heard by addressing individual complaints.

CMS identifies the core functions of the QIO Program as:

- Improving quality of care for beneficiaries
- Protecting the integrity of the Medicare Trust Fund by ensuring that Medicare pays only for services and goods that are reasonable and necessary and that are provided in the most appropriate setting
- Protecting beneficiaries by expeditiously addressing individual complaints, such as beneficiary complaints; provider-based notice appeals; violations of the Emergency Medical Treatment and Labor Act (EMTALA); and other related responsibilities as articulated in QIO-related law.

The CMS uses Clinical Quality Measures, or CQMs, to ensure that healthcare systems deliver effective, safe, efficient, patient-centered, equitable, and timely care. Clinical quality measures track the quality of healthcare services provided. They examine providers' ability to deliver high-quality care or relate to long-term goals for quality healthcare.

CQMs measure many aspects of patient care, including:

- Health outcomes
- Clinical processes
- Patient safety
- Efficient use of healthcare resources
- Care coordination
- Patient engagements
- Population and public health
- Adherence to clinical guidelines

Core Measures of the Centers for Medicare & Medicaid Services

CMS also identifies a set of care standards known as Core Measures. Core Measures are standards that have been shown through scientific evidence to improve patient outcomes, and they set the standard for care provided to patients while in the hospital.

As the healthcare system moves toward value-based reimbursement models, providers are required to report multiple quality measures to many different entities. To address this issue, CMS created the Core Quality Measures Collaborative, where CMS, commercial plans, Medicare and Medicaid managed plans, NQF, physicians, care provider organizations, and consumers work together to identify core sets of quality measures. The Core Quality Measures Collaborative established agreed-upon core measure sets that are coordinated across both government and commercial payers. Seven core measure sets were created, and can be viewed in the table on the following page.

More information on Core Measures and links to complete lists can be found at https://www.cms.gov/Medicare/Quality-Initiatives-Patient-Assessment-Instruments/ QualityMeasures/Core-Measures.html

Core Measure	Examples of Items Measured
Cardiology	• Therapy with aspirin, P2Y12 inhibitor, and statin at discharge following PCI in eligible patients • Primary PCI received within 90 minutes of hospital arrival
Accountable Care Organizations, Patient Centered Medical Homes, and Primary Care	• Persistent beta blocker treatment after a heart attack • Comprehensive diabetes care: eye exam, hemoglobin A1c (HbA1c) testing, foot exam, medical attention for nephropathy • Cervical cancer screening
Gastroenterology	• Age appropriate screening colonoscopy • Screening for Hepatocellular Carcinoma (HCC) in patients with Hepatitis C • One-time screening for Hepatitis C Virus (HCV) for patients at risk
HIV and Hepatitis C	• Pneumocystis jiroveci pneumonia (PCP) prophylaxis for HIV patients • HIV viral load suppression • One-time screening for Hepatitis C Virus (HCV) for patients at risk
Medical Oncology	• Patients with breast cancer and negative or undocumented human epidermal growth factor receptor 2 (HER2) status who are spared treatment with trastuzumab • Radical prostatectomy pathology reporting • Proportion of members receiving chemotherapy in the last 14 days of life
Obstetrics and Gynecology	• Breast cancer and cervical cancer screening • Exclusive breast milk feeding • Elective delivery and cesarean section rate
Orthopedics	• Hospital-level risk-standardized complication rate (RSCR) following elective primary total hip arthroplasty (THA) and/or total knee arthroplasty (TKA) • Patient experience with surgical care based on the Consumer Assessment of Healthcare Providers and Systems (CAHPS) Surgical Care Survey

AHRQ

The Agency for Healthcare Research and Quality (AHRQ) is part of the United States Department of Health and Human Services. The agency publishes and disseminates national clinical practice guidelines. Its mission is to produce evidence to make healthcare safer, higher quality, and more accessible, equitable, and affordable. The data used to measure performance include administrative data such as billing or claims data, medical record information, patient-derived data such as surveys, confidential reports from providers, and direct observation.

The Quality Indicators (QIs) established and maintained by the AHRQ are evidence-based and can be used to identify variations in the quality of care provided on both an inpatient and outpatient basis. The QIs consist of four models measuring various aspects of quality: Prevention Quality Indicators (PQIs), Inpatient Quality Indicators (IQIs), Patient Safety Indicators (PSIs), and Pediatric Indicators (PDIs).

Prevention Quality Indicators (PQIs) – Identifies conditions where good outpatient care can potentially prevent the need for hospitalization, or in which early intervention can prevent complications or increase in disease severity.

Examples of PQIs are:

- Hypertension admission rate
- Congestive heart failure admission rate
- Low birth weight rate
- Angina admission without procedure
- Uncontrolled diabetes admission rate

Inpatient Quality Indicators (IQIs) – Indicators reflecting the quality of care inside hospitals, including inpatient mortality; the utilization of procedures that are questionably misused, overused, or underused; and procedure volume where higher volume is associated with lower mortality.

Examples of the mortality indicators for inpatient surgical procedures include:

- Pancreatic resection mortality rate
- Abdominal aortic aneurysm (AAA) repair mortality rate
- Coronary artery bypass graft (CABG) mortality rate
- Hip replacement mortality rate

Examples of the mortality indicators for inpatient medical conditions include:

- Acute myocardial infarction (AMI) mortality rate
- Congestive heart failure mortality rate
- Hip fracture mortality rate
- Pneumonia mortality rate
- Examples of the procedure utilization indicators include:
- Primary cesarean delivery rate
- Vaginal birth after cesarean (VBAC) rate
- Laparoscopic cholecystectomy rate
- Incidental appendectomy in the elderly rate

Examples of the IQIs that focus on volume include:

- Pancreatic resection volume
- Abdominal aortic aneurysm (AAA) repair volume
- Coronary artery bypass graft (CABG) volume
- Carotid endarterectomy (CEA) volume

Patient Safety Indicators (PSIs) – Potentially preventable instances of complications and other iatrogenic events resulting from exposure to the healthcare system. There are currently 27 PSIs covering 2 levels: the provider level (within a hospital) and the area level (within a metropolitan service area or county).

Examples of provider-level PSIs include:

- Postoperative pulmonary embolism or deep vein thrombosis
- Postoperative respiratory failure
- Postoperative hemorrhage or hematoma
- Decubitus ulcer
- Foreign body left in during procedure
- Birth trauma – injury to neonate
- Obstetric trauma – cesarean section delivery
- Complications of anesthesia
- Transfusion reaction (AB/Rh)

Examples of the area-level PSIs include:

- Foreign body left in during procedure
- Selected infections due to medical care
- Postoperative wound dehiscence in abdominopelvic surgical patients
- Accidental puncture or laceration
- Transfusion reaction
- Postoperative hemorrhage or hematoma

Pediatric Quality Indicators (PDIs) – These indicators reflect the quality of care for neonates and children younger than 17 inside the hospital and identify potentially avoidable hospitalizations among children. There are currently 13 provider-level PDIs and 5 area-level PDIs.

Examples of provider-level PDIs include:

- Foreign body left in during procedure
- Iatrogenic pneumothorax in neonates
- Postoperative hemorrhage or hematoma
- Postoperative sepsis
- Transfusion reaction
- Examples of area-level PDIs are:
- Asthma admission rate
- Perforated appendix admission rate
- Urinary tract infection admission rate

More information on AHRQ and links to complete lists of their QIs can be found at http://www.ncbi.nlm.nih.gov/books/NBK2664/

Data Interpretation and Reporting

When interpreting data, validity and reliability must be taken into consideration. Validity refers to the meaningfulness of the data being measured; that is, is it measuring what it is intended to measure. Reliability refers to the accuracy. The case manager must ensure that data gathered is reliable by avoiding bias.

After data is collected it must be interpreted. This is the process of assigning meaning to information collected and determining the conclusions, significance, and implications of the findings. It is important once again to avoid any bias while interpreting the data. Information obtained during the data collection and interpretation is then reported.

As care coordinators, case managers must be able to show that the interventions implemented changed the patient's outcome. This information is shown in case management reports.

Several of the reports case managers use include:

- Patient care reports
- Quality improvement
- Cost benefit of case management services
- Justification to continue intervention
- Demonstrating lack of results with current intervention to justify approving more costly intervention

Patient Care reports

Patient reports are important, as this is where case managers document the value of case management involvement. By recording the patient's condition prior to case management, the goals of case management, the patient's current condition relative to the goals, and case management interventions, case managers are able to demonstrate the value they bring.

Example: At case opening client was unclear regarding his diagnosis. Case manager educated client regarding diagnosis. Client has a better understanding of his diagnosis and is now able to verbalize that understanding.

The frequency of patient reports may vary but should always be done at case closure. Patient reports may include:

- Justification for case management involvement, such as the diagnosis
- Desired outcomes and goals of case management
- Progress toward the outcomes
- Cost of care with case management intervention
- Cost of care without case management intervention
- Cost savings due to case management intervention

Quality Improvement reports

Items included in Quality Improvement reports include:

- Indicator being measured
- Case management intervention
- Measurement used to evaluate response to intervention
- Improvement in quality directly related to case management intervention

Cost Benefit reports

Cost benefit reports provide a summary of case management intervention and include:

- Diagnosis
- Summary of interventions
- Total time in case management
- Total cost without case management intervention
- Total cost with case management intervention
- Total cost savings

Justification of Continuation of Intervention

Some interventions need documentation of progress for continuation. In these cases, provide:

- Data from before the intervention was initiated
- Current data
- Goal of intervention

The following is an example for a patient receiving physical therapy.

- Data before initiating intervention: Ambulates 12 feet with wheeled walker and max assist.

- Current data: Ambulates 100 feet with straight cane and stands by assist.
- Goal of intervention: Ambulate 250 feet independently with least restrictive assistive device.

Justify More Costly Intervention

When the current intervention does not produce the desired results, the case manager may alert the patient care team so an alternative plan of care can be proposed. If the cost of the new proposed plan of care is more expensive than the current plan of care, the case manager must document the rationale for the new plan. In this instance he or she must provide:

- Prior data
- Data from current therapy showing minimal or no progress
- Duration of current intervention
- Cost of current intervention
- Proposed intervention
- Cost of proposed intervention
- Duration of proposed intervention
- Goal of proposed intervention

Cost-Benefit Analysis

A cost-benefit report formally documents monetary savings related to case management involvement. There are two types of savings: hard cost savings and soft cost savings.

Savings directly related to the case manager's actions are hard savings.

Examples of hard savings include:

- Transfer to a lower level of care
- Decrease in length of stay

- Negotiation to a lower rate for a service

- Change to an in-network provider

Soft cost savings are potential savings and are more difficult to measure than hard savings. Soft cost savings are costs avoided due to case management intervention. These may include:

- Avoided hospital readmission

- Prevention of medical complications

- Avoided ER visits

There is a formula to calculate cost savings. First, the cost of service with case management involvement (Actual Cost) is added to the cost of the case management service. This number is then subtracted from the cost of intervention without case management involvement (Potential Cost). The difference is the cost savings associated with case management involvement.

Cost savings = Potential Costs - (Actual Cost + Cost of Case Management)

In addition to documenting the effectiveness of case management, a cost-benefit report can be used to justify an Alternative Treatment Plan (ATP) or to compare costs of various treatment options.

Program Evaluation and Research Methods

Case management programs must be evaluated for effectiveness in reaching the desired outcomes and goals. This gives insight into what is working and what needs modified. Two ways to evaluate the effectiveness of the case management program are to conduct surveys and to measure outcomes.

Case Management Satisfaction Survey

The patient can be surveyed for satisfaction at any point in a case management program, but all patients should be surveyed when their cases are closed. The survey must be objective and evaluate the quality and effectiveness of the case management program. The results of the survey provide the patient's perspective and value of case management. To receive the most honest answers to the survey, the patient should be allowed to remain anonymous if so desired.

Survey results have multiple purposes. They may be used for marketing purposes, or they can be used in quality assurance, showing where goals are met, and where training, process improvement, or other intervention needs to take place.

Case Management Outcomes

Clinical outcomes can be measured on groups of patients, such as patients with a specific disease or those requiring a particular service (e.g., hospitalization, home health), as well as individual cases. The outcomes measured depend on the setting in which case management is provided.

Examples of outcomes measured include:
- Percentage of patients readmitted to the hospital within 30 days
- Percentage of patients adherent to the treatment plan
- Average length of the hospital stay
- Percentage of clients who returned to work
- Percentage of clients who maintained hemoglobin A1C <9

Healthcare Analytics

Health Risk Assessments, Predictive Modeling, and Adjusted Clinical Groups are tools to identify at-risk individuals who may benefit from case management services. The goal is to be proactive and provide services to prevent disease, complications, morbidity, mortality, and hospitalization, therefore reducing cost and improving quality of life.

Health Risk Assessment

The Health Risk Assessment (HRA) is a tool to assess a patient's health status, risk of negative health outcomes, and readiness to change certain behaviors. It is used to design a prevention plan, so the patient can take action to improve his or her health status and delay or prevent the onset of disease caused by reported at-risk behaviors.

There are three components to the HRA: the questionnaire, the risk calculation, and feedback. The questionnaire is a self-reported assessment that identifies health behaviors and risk factors known only to the patient, such as physical activity, dietary habits, and smoking. It may also include biometrics.

The table below shows information often included in the health risk assessment.

Category	Data
Demographic Data	Sex, age
Biometric Assessment	Height, weight, blood pressure, cholesterol, blood sugar
Lifestyle	Physical activity/exercise, smoking, alcohol intake, diet, seat belt use
Family Medical History	Cancer, diabetes, hypertension, hypercholesterolemia

To calculate the patient's risk, the healthcare provider reviews the questionnaire responses and biometric data, assesses the patient's health status, and evaluates the risk of developing certain diseases, disabilities, or injuries.

The third component to the HRA is the personalized feedback aimed at reducing risk factors. The healthcare provider suggests appropriate interventions and provides motivation to change unhealthy or at-risk behaviors.

HRAs do more than just evaluate risk for disease or disability, and they are sometimes referred to as health assessments or wellness profiles. HRAs are also used by employers for wellness programs, by fitness centers to screen members before using equipment, and by health insurance companies to identify individuals for disease management programs.

HRAs are also used during Medicaid enrollment to identify individuals with health problems that need immediate attention. The Affordable Care Act specifies that an HRA be part of the annual wellness visit for Medicare beneficiaries. The ACA also specifies that the HRA must identify chronic diseases, injury risk, modifiable risk factors, and urgent health needs.

Though the HRA is an important tool, there are some limitations and methodological concerns. The most obvious is that self-reporting can lead to inaccurate information, due to a patient's recall bias, lack of understanding of the questions, or reluctance to report socially unacceptable behaviors. In addition, factors such as language, culture, and literacy level can affect the results.

Predictive Modeling

Predictive modeling uses technology and statistical methods to analyze enormous amounts of data to predict outcomes for individual patients. A model can be simple or complex, but more complex models are more accurate in predicting outcomes. Most often the data comes from health plan claims and identifies patterns of physician, specialist, laboratory, pharmaceutical, ER, and hospital care.

The data is compiled, analyzed, and interpreted to proactively identify individuals who are in danger of developing a high-risk disease. The objective is to identify these high-risk individuals at the earliest opportunity and to begin implementing appropriate interventions. This allows for healthcare resources to be targeted toward those who can benefit most.

Predictive modeling can be a critical tool in managing future resource consumption. It identifies individuals whose future medical expenses could be significant and provides appropriate education and intervention through a disease management or case management program. This improves use of case management resources by focusing them on patients who need assistance. This early intervention also increases opportunities for success, decreases adverse outcomes, and brings costs under control.

Adjusted Clinical Group (ACG)

The Adjusted Clinical Group (ACG) System is a tool developed by Johns Hopkins University to assess risk. It uses the diagnostic and pharmaceutical code information from insurance claims and electronic medical records to measuring morbidity in large populations based on disease patterns, age, and gender. It provides an accurate representation of the morbidity burden of populations, subgroups, or individual patients based on the overall picture, and not on individual diseases. This information is used to evaluate provider performance more accurately and fairly, set equitable payment rates, forecast healthcare utilization, and identify patients at high risk.

Unlike many traditional methods of identifying clients for case management, such as emergency department usage, hospitalization, or high dollar claims, the ACG Predictive Model identifies individuals who are likely to become high resource users. By focusing on developing patterns of morbidity, such as those seeing multiple providers and taking multiple prescriptions, it identifies individuals who can benefit from case management and care coordination earlier.

Caseload Calculation

Many factors determine the caseload capacity of a case manager. A case manager who conducts face-to-face case management in a rural area cannot manage the same caseload as a telephonic case manager, due to logistical and transportation factors. And complex cases require more time and involvement from the case manager than disease management cases, for example.

Because of the multiple factors and complexity of determining an appropriate caseload, the Case Management Society of America (CMSA) created a Case Load Capacity Calculator tool (http://clcc.cm-innovators.com/). This online tool is open for public use after registering. It takes into account several factors to determine the appropriate caseload for a case manager.

These factors include:

- Profession (nurse/social worker)
- Setting (clinic, hospital, subacute, health plan, workers' compensation)
- Other roles the case manager performs (behavioral health, utilization management, disease management, supervisory roles, preceptor/trainer)
- Complexity of cases
- Experience of case manager
- Length of time in current role
- Site-based technology (hand-written reports, one information technology system, multiple information technology systems)
- Types of contact (face-to-face, telephonic)
- Non-case management activities (meetings, continuing education, travel, training)

Additional Resources

Quality and Performance Improvement Concepts

HCAHPS: Patients' Perspectives of Care Survey - Centers for Medicare & Medicaid Services: https://www.cms.gov/Medicare/Quality-Initiatives-Patient-Assessment-instruments/HospitalQualityInits/HospitalHCAHPS.html

HCAHPS Hospital Survey: http://www.hcahpsonline.org/home.aspx

Quality Indicators, Techniques and Applications

DMAIC Methodology/A Six Sigma Process Improvement Method: http://www.villanovau.com/resources/six-sigma/six-sigma-methodology-dmaic/#.V4zZ7o7zcgV

Lean: http://transitionconsultants.com/uncategorized/lean-pages

Healthcare Analytics

Health Risk Assessment: http://www.cdc.gov/policy/hst/hra/frameworkforhra.pdf

Health Risk Assessments CDC: https://www.cms.gov/Medicare/Coverage/CoverageGenInfo/downloads/healthriskassessmentsCDCfinal.pdf

Health Risk Assessments - Medicaid and CHIP Child Core Set Manual: https://www.medicaid.gov/Medicaid-CHIP-Program-Information/By-Topics/Quality-of-Care/Downloads/Medicaid-and-CHIP-Child-Core-Set-Manual.pdf

Accreditation Standards and Requirements

Joint Commission: http://www.jointcommission.org/benefits_of_joint_commission_accreditation/

URAC - About URAC: https://www.urac.org/about-urac/about-urac/

URAC - Case Management Standards: https://www.urac.org/wp-content/uploads/CaseMgmt-Standards-At-A-Glance-10-9-2013.pdf

URAC - Accreditation: https://www.urac.org/accreditation-and-measurement/accreditation-and-measurement/

CARF: http://www.carf.org/Accreditation/

Core Measures: https://www.cms.gov/Medicare/Quality-Initiatives-Patient-Assessment-Instruments/QualityMeasures/Core-Measures.html

AHRQ: http://www.ncbi.nlm.nih.gov/books/NBK2664/

NCQA: https://www.ncqa.org/Portals/0/Programs/Accreditation/case%20mgmt-5_8.2.12.pdf

NQF - Measures, Reports & Tools: http://www.qualityforum.org/Measures_Reports_Tools.aspx

Chapter Four:
Rehabilitation Concepts
and Strategies

Case managers need to have an understanding of levels of care in rehabilitative treatment as well as adaptive equipment and assistive devices for a variety of illnesses and disabilities. They also need to be familiar with basic elements of vocational rehabilitation.

Assistive Devices

Assistive Devices and Technologies

Assistive devices and assistive technology devices are tangible items or pieces of equipment that aid a person with a disability in carrying out a task. Use of the device allows the individual with impaired abilities or functional limitations greater independence in performing activities. They can be high-tech, such as computers and hearing aids, or as simple as a cane or reacher. The purpose of the device is to improve function and independence. They can also be used as job accommodations.

Aids for physical disabilities that affect mobility include:

- Canes
- Crutches
- Walkers
- Scooters
- Manual wheelchairs
- Power wheelchairs

Computer software and hardware can allow use of computers to people with sensory or motor impairments. This includes:

- Alternate keyboard
- Voice recognition programs
- Screen readers
- Screen enlargement applications

Devices to assist with orientation to person, place, and time include:

- Clocks
- Calendars
- Smart phones

- Memory books
- Location devices

A prosthetic device is an artificial substitute or replacement part for a missing or impaired part of the body and includes:

- Hip, knee, or other joint replacement
- Lens replacement following cataract surgery
- Breast implants following mastectomy
- Tooth
- Eye
- Artificial arm or leg

Telecommunication devices for the deaf (TDD) include:

- Teletypewriter (TTY)
- Text Telephone Device (TTD)

The acronyms TDD, TTY, and TTD are used interchangeably to refer to any type of text-based telecommunications equipment used by someone with hearing or speech difficulties. Both the sender and the receiver of the message need the equipment.

There are also relay services to allow a hearing impaired person with a TDD to communicate with another party who does not have a TDD. The operator at the relay service uses TDD equipment to communicate with the hearing impaired person, and a telephone to communicate with the other party, acting like an interpreter. There are also video relay services that allow the hearing impaired person to communicate in American Sign Language. The popularity of cell phones and texting has made communication for the deaf much easier, as no special equipment is needed.

Other types of assistive devices include:

- Hearing aids
- Page-turners
- Book-holders
- Adapted pencil grips
- Closed captioning
- Reachers

There are several points to consider when helping a client choose a mobility device (that is, a manual wheelchair, power wheelchair, or scooter). It is important to understand the client's insurance coverage for the various devices, such as the criteria for medical necessity and coverage for maintenance and repairs.

Manual wheelchairs are the least expensive and are lightweight, making them much more portable than power chairs. On the other hand, they require sufficient upper-body strength to self-propel, making them unsuitable for some clients.

For clients who are unable to self-propel, a scooter or power wheelchair can be a better option. Power wheelchairs offer the greatest variety of options and accessories to customize the chair to the needs of the client, but they can be much more expensive than manual wheelchairs. They also tend to be very heavy, requiring the use of a power lift for transport. Scooters are often faster but provide less stability than power wheelchairs. Many scooters can disassemble quickly for transport.

Both scooters and power wheelchairs are battery operated and require regular charging and maintenance. Before purchasing a scooter or power chair, the client should be evaluated by a physical therapist to ensure he or she will be able to use the device.

Rehabilitation After Hospitalization or an Acute Health Condition

Following a prolonged hospitalization or an acute illness or injury, such as a stroke or hip fracture, patients are at risk of experiencing a significant loss of functioning. This risk is increased in critically ill patients, patients with complications or long-term intensive care stays, patients with disabilities or pre-existing chronic conditions, and the elderly. Early identification of rehabilitation needs and proactive rehabilitation can reduce healthcare costs. Rehabilitation can occur at the acute-level hospital, the non-acute inpatient setting, or in the community.

See Vocational and Rehabilitation Service Delivery Systems for more information on care settings.

Assessment of Physical Functioning

The functional assessment is an important part of rehabilitation. It guides the treatment types and duration, measures outcomes, estimates the amount of care to be provided by others, and provides documentation for payment for care. The Functional Independence Measures instrument (FIM) assesses adult inpatients, while the WeeFIM is used for children.

Functional Independence Measures Instrument (FIM)

FIM is used in the inpatient rehab setting and measures the individual's level of independence/dependence in the areas of:

- Self-care (eating, grooming, bathing, upper body dressing, lower body dressing)
- Toileting (bladder control, sphincter control)
- Transfers (bed/chair/wheelchair, toilet, tub/shower)

- Locomotion (walk, wheelchair, stairs)
- Communication (comprehension, expression)
- Social cognition (social interaction, problem solving, memory)

Clinicians score patients from 1-7, with 7 indicating complete independence and 1 indicating total assist from another person.

WeeFIM

The WeeFIM assesses children in the same areas as the FIM and uses the same rating scale. It is used for children without disabilities ages 6 months to 7 years, and in children with developmental disabilities ages 6 months to 12 years.

Vocational and Rehabilitation Service Delivery Systems

Inpatient Rehabilitation

Inpatient rehabilitation may be provided in a medical hospital, a freestanding inpatient rehabilitation hospital, or a skilled nursing facility. The setting is determined by the client's medical and functional status and the level of care the facility can provide.

The medical hospital level is for patients with an acute medical need that requires ongoing medical care. Rehabilitations such as physical therapy, occupational therapy, speech therapy, and cognitive rehabilitation are provided, but medical care is the priority. This level of care can be delivered in two hospital settings: acute care hospital or long term acute care hospital.

The inpatient rehabilitation hospital provides intense, multidisciplinary therapy to patients with a functional loss due to factors such as injury, illness, or deconditioning. The primary focus is to restore the client to self-sufficiency or maximum possible functional independence. These hospitals utilize an interdisciplinary team to provide intensive rehabilitation in the areas of physical therapy, occupational therapy, speech therapy, cognitive therapy, respiratory therapy, psychology services, and/or prosthetic/orthotic services. To qualify for this level of care, patients must be able to tolerate a minimum of 3 hours of therapy per day, 5 to 7 days per week, and be medically stable.

Skilled nursing facilities (SNF) provide rehabilitation services such as physical therapy, occupational therapy, and speech therapy, at a less intense level than inpatient rehabilitation hospitals. Patients who need rehabilitation after injury or hospitalization but cannot tolerate 3 hours of therapy per day may benefit from the SNF level of rehabilitation. Patients must be medically stable to qualify for SNF care.

Community Rehabilitation

Patients who do not require the inpatient level of care can still benefit from rehabilitation services utilizing outpatient rehabilitation or home health services.

Day program – An outpatient program for patients who no longer require hospitalization but still need intensive, coordinated rehabilitation for several hours per day.

Outpatient rehabilitation – Patients travel to a clinic or hospital to attend sessions and return home the same day. Typically, a therapy session lasts from 30 minutes to an hour.

Home health – Therapy is provided in the patient's home for up to one hour per discipline per visit. Visits are usually made up to three times per week. To qualify for home health care, the patient must be homebound, meaning taxing effort is required to leave the home. A person may leave home for medical treatment or short, infrequent non-medical reasons, such as attending religious services.

Vocational Rehabilitation

Vocational rehabilitation is a federal-state, eligibility-based, career development program. It provides a wide range of individualized services to eligible individuals with disabilities. The individuals acquire skills, attitudes, and resources needed to obtain and keep a job. The vocational rehabilitation program, unlike any other federal or state jobs program, is highly individualized. Vocational rehabilitation counselors meet with eligible individuals and together they determine patients' vocational objectives.

To be eligible for vocational rehabilitation services, federal regulations require the individual to be disabled and to be able to benefit from vocational rehabilitation services. The disability must be a physical or mental impairment that is a substantial barrier to employment. Those receiving Supplemental Security Income (SSI) and/or Social Security Disability Insurance (SSDI) are presumed eligible unless their disabilities are too severe for them to benefit from vocational rehabilitation (defined as being unable to achieve employment).

Supported Employment

Supported employment is paid, competitive employment in an integrated setting with ongoing support for individuals with the most severe disabilities (e.g., psychiatric or intellectual disability, significant learning disabilities, traumatic brain injury, deafness and blindness, extreme mobility impairments, and other most severe disabilities). Because of the nature and severity of these disabilities, workers need on-going support services in order to obtain, perform, and retain their jobs. Supported employment provides assistance such as job coaching, job placement, specialized job training, on-site assistive technology training, help interacting with employers, and individually tailored supervision.

Supported employment provides a vehicle for eligible individuals to enter competitive employment, where they would otherwise be unable to do so due to the impact of their disabling conditions.

Rehabilitation Post-Injury, Including Work-Related

In the event of a work-related injury, the goal is always to return the client to work as quickly as possible. A vocational case manager can use several tools to achieve this goal. The functional assessment is an important part of rehabilitation, as it guides the treatment types and duration, measures outcomes, estimates the amount of care to be provided by others, and provides documentation for payment for care.

The Functional Capacity Assessment (FCA) is used to directly measure a person's functional ability to perform specific work-related tasks. The case manager may conduct a job analysis to identify accommodations that would allow the employee to return to the job.

If the client has reached Medical Maximum Improvement (MMI) and cannot perform the essential duties of the job, with or without accommodation, a Transferable Skills Analysis can be completed to document current and projected employment based on the skills, abilities, and aptitude of the client. A Vocational Evaluation can be completed to determine the client's work capacity and potential for vocational rehabilitation.

If the medical case manager determines the client may need vocational case management (aka vocational rehabilitation) to assist with job development or placement after an injury, he or she should make or obtain a referral. The vocational case manager will then perform a vocational assessment and job analysis, assessing for transferable skills, and arrange for vocational testing if necessary. He or she will create a vocational rehabilitation plan to assist the client in obtaining employment.

Job Analysis

A functional job analysis is the process of collecting data to define a person's job requirements and essential and nonessential job duties. This data can be collected from interviews with workers and supervisors, on-site observations, and analysis of company job descriptions. It provides detailed information related to major tasks, as well as the physical, cognitive, and behavioral capacities required to perform the job. Items examined in the job analysis may include: essential duties of the job, tools and equipment used, and amount of time spent standing, walking, sitting, operating a vehicle, climbing, reaching, bending, kneeling, and lifting. Along with specific tasks, the job analysis also includes details regarding scheduling, location, equipment needed, and required competencies.

In rehabilitation, the goal of the job analysis is to identify essential job functions and requirements to satisfactorily perform the work. Job requirements must be the focus, not the individual worker's skills.

Essential job functions are the basic duties fundamental to the job, and the employee must be able to perform them with or without reasonable accommodations. The most obvious functions are those the position exists to perform. For example, an obvious job function for a cashier is to exchange money with customers. Other criteria for determining essential job functions include a reference in the written job description, the amount of time spent performing the function, and the consequences if this employee is not required to perform a particular function.

The job analysis may be performed by one discipline or an interdisciplinary rehabilitation team. Disciplines that often perform rehabilitation job analysis include:

- Physical therapists
- Occupational therapists
- Vocational rehabilitation specialists
- Ergonomists

Functional Capacity Evaluation

The Functional Capacity Evaluation (FCE) is used to directly measure the patient's physical ability to perform work-related activities. The worker is examined as he or she completes activities, directly measuring the physical level of work the individual can perform. It is an objective tool that is dependent on the motivation, cognitive awareness, and sincerity of effort of the participant and only reflects what he or she is able or willing to do at the time of the evaluation. Factors that may influence this include sincerity of effort, motivation, and mental alertness.

The FCE is a comprehensive exam, covering all physical demands required of the employee. It can be part of the initial assessment, used to determine the work conditioning plan, or to reassess progress and the ability to return to work. Along with assessing the capacity for returning to the current job, it can also be used to assess for a job modification or a new job. The FCE is done in a structured setting, not the place of work, and is performed by an independent physical therapist, occupational therapist, or physician, not the treating clinician.

An FCE may be indicated when:
- There is potential for re-injury
- Rehabilitation findings are inconsistent
- It is a complicated case
- Time off work exceeds guidelines

During the FCE the patient is evaluated as he performs activities required for his job. This may include, but is not limited to:
- Squatting
- Sitting
- Pushing
- Pulling

- Turning
- Standing
- Kneeling
- Balancing
- Navigating stairs
- Hand grip

The amount of time the patient requires to perform each of these tasks is important.

Work Hardening and Work Conditioning

An employee who has recovered from his or her injury may need work conditioning or work hardening to be able to return to pre-injury duties.

Work hardening is an individualized, intense, highly structured program designed to return the worker to full employment. It is done 3-5 days per week in a real or simulated work setting under the direction of a multidisciplinary team. Real or simulated work tasks are combined with conditioning activities, with the goal to improve the injured worker's biomechanical, neuromuscular, cardiovascular-metabolic, and psychosocial functioning. The hardening ensures that muscles are conditioned specifically for the job-related tasks to be undertaken by the worker. Productivity, safety, physical tolerance, and work behaviors are also addressed. The program is individualized to the client based on his or her injury or impairment and job description. It states the amount of lifting, bending, stretching, or other activities required to perform the job duties. A job analysis or on-site observation of the worker's job may be performed to identify goals related to job functions. The purpose is to maximize the employee's ability to return to work safely, with less likelihood of re-injury.

Work conditioning aims to restore function so the client can return to work. It is done under the direction of a physical therapist in a therapy setting 2-4 times per week. Work conditioning differs from work hardening in that the focus is not on specific tasks the client must perform (for example, lifting a 20-pound box and placing it on a shelf), but rather on building the strength required to lift anything.

Work Adjustment

The focus of work adjustment is on attitude and behavioral and social skills for clients with behavioral health issues. Work adjustment can be done individually or in a group setting. Real or simulated work activity is performed under close supervision at a rehabilitation facility or work setting. The goal is to improve problems that prevent the client from obtaining employment, such as attendance, punctuality, hygiene, or interpersonal relationship skills. Work adjustment might be used after a traumatic brain injury, for example, wherein the worker has developed behavioral issues.

Comparison of Work Hardening, Work Conditioning, and Work Adjustment

Work Conditioning	Work Hardening	Work Adjustment
2-4 days per week	3-5 days per week	Varies
Done in therapy setting	In real or simulated work setting	Rehabilitation facility or work setting
Goal is to restore function	Goal is to return to work	Goal is to improve problems preventing employment
Less intense than work hardening	More intense than work conditioning	Focuses on attitude and behavioral and social skills
For physical injury	For physical injury	For behavioral health issues

Transitional Work Duty

After a work injury, an employee may need some assistance before he is able to return to the job duties he had prior to the injury. If he is able to work but at a lower capacity than before the injury, the worker may be a candidate for Transitional Work Duty (TWD). This would be appropriate for a police officer who broke his leg, for example. He is able to work, but not in his normal job function. He could be placed in a desk job until he is able to return to his normal job duties.

TWD allows an injured employee to return to productive work with their employer while under the care of rehabilitation professionals. The employer creates a value-added temporary position based on the knowledge and skills of the employee. The work must conform to the restrictions put in place by the employee's treating physician. Only employees with temporary injuries who will eventually be able to return to their normal full-time duties are eligible for TWD.

Job Development and Placement Related to Workers' Compensation

After a work-related injury, the goal is for the worker to achieve maximum medical improvement and to return to work as soon as possible. The return to work options are evaluated in the following order:

1. Same job, same employer

2. Modified job, same employer

3. Different job, same employer, using transferable skills

4. Same job, different employer

5. Different job, different employer, using transferable skills

6. Training for different job with same or different employer

7. Self-employment

Vocational Aspects of Chronic Illness and Disability

The vocational aspects of a chronic illness or disability can be a challenge to manage. Along with medical and psychological issues, the reduction or loss of income can place a huge burden on the client and his or her family. Clients usually exhaust any paid time off first. If the client is expected to be out of work for an extended period of time, he or she will want to apply for protection under the Family and Medical Leave Act (FMLA). FMLA is not a source of income, but it does protect the employee's job.

Workers' compensation clients have an advantage over clients who suffer from an illness: They are afforded benefits to get them through. Persons who are injured outside of work or suffering a prolonged illness can lose their medical and other benefits, as well as their income, if they cannot return to work or be approved for disability.

According to the U.S. Department of Health and Human Services, the employment rate for adults with disabilities is significantly lower than for those without disabilities. The most frequently reported reasons for difficulty in obtaining employment are lack of available, appropriate jobs, followed by lack of transportation. Many individuals need some accommodation, such as accessible parking or transportation, elevators, or specially designed workstations.

The Ticket to Work Program exists for clients aged 18 to 64 who want to return to work but currently receive Social Security benefits based on disability under the Social Security Disability Insurance (SSDI) program and/or the Supplemental Security Income (SSI) program. It is a voluntary program that provides expanded options for accessing employment services, vocational rehabilitation services, or other support services needed to enter, maintain, and advance in employment. These services include training, career counseling, vocational rehabilitation, job placement, and ongoing support services necessary to achieve a work goal. The ultimate goal of the program is to eliminate the need for Social Security disability cash benefits, while allowing the client to maintain his or her Medicare or Medicaid benefits.

More information can be found at https://yourtickettowork.com/web/ttw

Job Modification/Job Accommodation

The terms job modification and job accommodation are often used interchangeably. To differentiate, however, a job modification is an across-the-board change to the job description, targeting skills. Examples include restructuring the job, eliminating marginal job functions, sharing job duties, or modifying company policy. Job accommodations are more individualized and focus on access. Examples include voice recognition software or an adjustable height desk to accommodate a wheelchair. Because most of the literature, as well as most case managers, use either accommodation or modification to mean both, the term accommodation will be used for the remainder of this section.

Accommodation Process

- Request accommodation: The person with the disability is responsible for requesting the accommodation.

- Identify functional limitations: Determine where the functional limitations intersect with the job duties; that is, which tasks the person cannot perform without accommodation.

- Identify accommodations: Discuss options with the employee. Often the accommodation is obvious or something the employee has used before successfully, but creative collaboration, extensive investigation, or outside assistance may be needed.

- Determine reasonable solutions: The ADA requires employers to provide reasonable accommodations for qualified applicants or employees with disabilities, unless doing so would cause undue hardship for the employer. Undue hardship can refer to accommodations that cause financial difficulty, are disruptive to the workplace, or fundamentally change the operation of the business.

- Make accommodation: The employee's preferences should be taken into account, but ultimately the employer will determine which accommodation is put into effect based on cost, business feasibility, and effectiveness.
- Monitor effectiveness: If the desired outcome is not achieved, the employee and employer should start the process again.

The Job Accommodations Network (JAN) is a consulting service provided by the U.S. Department of Labor's Office of Disability Employment Policy (ODEP) that provides free information on job accommodations. JAN's website states, "Working toward practical solutions that benefit both employer and employee, JAN helps people with disabilities enhance their employability, and shows employers how to capitalize on the value and talent that people with disabilities add to the workplace."

Data collected on the cost of accommodations show that more than half of all accommodations cost nothing. For modifications that do have a cost, the majority are under $500, and tax incentives and funding are available through several organizations to help offset the expense.

Accommodations are not limited to adjustment or modifications of physical equipment. The Americans with Disabilities Act lists these six categories of accommodations:

- Job restructuring – Adjustments to work procedures
- Assistive devices – Equipment that helps the employee complete the task
- Training – Helps an employee learn or relearn job duties
- Personal assistant – A person who helps an employee with job duties
- Building modification – Alterations to the physical environment that allow equal access to the facility
- Job reassignment – Temporary or permanent transfer of task assignment, or sharing jobs with other employees

Additional Resources

Ticket to Work

https://yourtickettowork.com/web/ttw

Job Accommodation Network

https://askjan.org/

United States Department of Labor

https://www.dol.gov/odep/resources/jan.htm

Chapter Five:
Ethical, Legal and Practice Standards

Case managers are licensed professionals who are obligated to work within ethical, legal, and practice standards as required by their license, governing bodies, and accrediting organizations. The board-certified case manager must have a good understanding of these standards; therefore, the Commission for Case Management Certification (CCMC) dedicates 15% of the CCM Exam to this topic.

Because of the board-certified case manager's role in protecting the rights, dignity, and public interest of his or her clients, the CCMC now requires CCMs to earn ethics-related continuing education credits for recertification.

Ethics Related to Care Delivery and Professional Practice

Ethical dilemmas occur when there is no "right" answer. Many circumstances can cause ethical issues for case managers, including, but not limited to:

- Dual masters (e.g., client/employer, client/provider, client/payer)
- Client advocacy vs. cost saving
- Case manager's influence on the client
- Client's values conflicting with case manager's values
- Client autonomy vs. client safety
- Client advocacy vs. family/caregiver wishes
- Advance directives
- Surrogate decision-making
- Refusal of treatment

To be an ethical dilemma, three conditions must be present.

- There is a decision the individual must make.
- There must be different courses of action to choose from.
- No matter which course of action is taken, an ethical principle is compromised.

With the advances of medical intervention, end of life care is rife with potential ethical dilemmas, ranging from the use of heroic measures to sustain life to assisted suicide. Other ethical issues at end of life can be related to advance directives, pain control, prolonging life, avoiding prolonged suffering, artificial nutrition and hydration, and forgoing treatment.

Experimental treatments also come with great potential for ethical issues. An ethical review committee should evaluate experimental treatments before they are offered to a patient. The committee will determine if the anticipated social value justifies possible harm. Any patient receiving experimental treatment must give informed consent after all aspects of care, including the likelihood of harm and the severity of the harm, are disclosed. There must also be an equitable system to select patients to participate in the experimental treatment.

The Case Management Society of America has developed a Code of Ethics to direct case managers through ethical dilemmas. According to their Standards of Practice, case managers are to behave and practice ethically, adhering to the tenets of the code of ethics that underlies their professional credential (e.g., nursing, social work, rehabilitation counseling, etc.). Case management ethics are demonstrated in the following ways:

- Primary obligation is to the client
- Respectful relationships with coworkers, employers, and other professionals
- Recognition that laws, rules, policies, insurance benefits, and regulations are sometimes in conflict with ethical principles; in such situations, case managers are bound to address such conflicts to the best of their abilities or to seek appropriate consultation
- Awareness of the five basic ethical principles and how they are applied: beneficence, non-malfeasance, autonomy, justice, and fidelity

The role of the case manager as a client advocate stems from the principle of client autonomy. The needs of the client, as the client sees them, are primary. The case manager collaborates with the autonomous client with the goal of fostering and encouraging the client's independence and self-determination. This involves informing the client of his options and supporting his decisions.

Understanding the underlying values and principles of case management is important in resolving ethical dilemmas, whether they are related to end of life issues, experimental treatments, refusal of care, or any other reason. Case management values are based on the belief that it is a means for improving client health, wellness, and autonomy through advocacy, communication, education, identification of service resources, and service facilitation.

The underlying principles of case management are:

- Placing public interest above one's own at all times
- Respecting the rights and inherent dignity of all clients
- Maintaining objectivity in relationships with clients
- Acting with integrity in dealing with other professionals to facilitate maximum benefit for the client
- Maintaining a level of competency that ensures each client will receive services appropriate and consistent for the client's conditions and circumstances
- Obeying laws and regulations

More information on professional conduct for case managers can be found on the CCMC's website: http://ccmcertification.org/sites/default/files/downloads/2012/Code%20of%20Professional%20Conduct%20for%20Case%20Managers.pdf

Standards of Practice

The case manager is held to numerous sets of standards, including:

- Commission for Case Manager Certification Code of Professional Conduct for Case Managers, revised January 2015
- Case Management Society of America's Standards of Practice for Case Management
- Other professional standards related to their licenses (for social workers or registered nurses, for example)
- State practice acts

The Commission for Case Manager Certification Code of Professional Conduct for Case Managers covers five areas:

- The Client Advocate
- Professional Responsibility, comprising competence and conflict of interest as well as other areas

- Case Manager/Client Relationships, including description of services, relationships with clients, and termination of services
- Confidentiality, Privacy, Security, and Recordkeeping
- Professional Relationships, including dual relationships, unprofessional behavior, fees, solicitation, and research

The entire CCMC Code of Professional Conduct for Case Managers can be found on the organization's website: https://ccmcertification.org/about-us/about-case-management/guidelines-practice. Below is a general overview.

Board-certified case managers are to serve as client advocates, perform comprehensive assessments to identify needs, and offer options when appropriate. They have a professional responsibility to practice within the boundaries of their role and competence and to participate in ongoing professional development. Any conflict of interest must be fully disclosed to all affected parties, and if any objection is made, the board-certified case manager will withdraw from further participation in the case.

Board-certified case managers are to maintain objectivity in their professional relationships and not impose their values on their clients. Prior to the termination of case management service, board-certified case managers will document notification of discontinuation to all relevant parties. They must also be knowledgeable about and act in accordance with all laws related to their scope of practice. Confidentiality must be maintained regarding the client's protected health information, including storage and disposal of records.

Any dual relationship that exists between the board-certified case manager and the client, payer, employer, friend, relative, research study, and/or other entities must be disclosed. Board-certified case managers may not participate in unprofessional behavior, such as failing to maintain appropriate professional boundaries with the client, disclosing information about a client via social media, committing a crime, and/or engaging in fraud, deceit, or discrimination.

The Case Management Society of America (CMSA) Standards of Practice for Case Managers is being updated at the time of this writing. Check the organization's website for the most up-to-date version at http://www.cmsa.org/ The CMSA Standards of Practice apply to all case managers and are not limited to members of CMSA.

Case Recording and Documentation

The importance of good documentation cannot be overemphasized. A case manager's documentation assists in clinical management, justifies interventions and expenses, and defends against claims of negligence. When documenting, case managers should maintain professional objectivity and document facts, recording quotations when appropriate. Opinions and biases should not be included in the medical record. The best time to document is during or right after the encounter.

What should be documented depends on the setting in which the case manager works. Examples may include, but are not limited to, records of:

- Acceptance or refusal of case management services
- Assessments
- Observations
- Monitoring
- Evaluation findings
- Interventions
- Progress with the current treatment
- Modifications to the case management plan, including rationale for the modifications
- Outcomes
- Discharge planning

- Medical stability of the patient within 24 hours of hospital discharge
- Plan of care, including patient/family agreement of
- Patient/family education
- Evidence of continuation of care after discharge from inpatient setting
- Informed consent
- Pre-certifications for procedures
- Advance directives

Additionally, all communication with the following must be documented:

- Patient
- Family
- Insurer/payer
- Vendors
- Other healthcare providers, both inside and outside the organization

Privacy and Confidentiality

A case manager must follow federal, state, and local laws regarding client privacy and confidentiality, as well as employer policies and case management standards of practice. At the beginning of the case manager/client relationship, case managers are to inform their clients that although their conversations are confidential, certain information obtained through the relationship may be disclosed to third parties including payers, service providers, and government authorities. The information shared is limited to what is necessary and relevant.

The case manager's client records kept in any form, including written, recorded, computerized, or stored on other medium, must be maintained in a manner to ensure confidentiality. When destroying these records, it must be done in a manner ensuring preservation of confidentiality.

HIPAA, the Health Insurance Portability and Accountability Act, covers protected health information that is released, transferred, or divulged outside the agency.

When can confidentiality be broken?

- When there is a duty to warn, such as to protect the patient or another party from harm
- After receiving a written authorization from the patient
- To comply with a court order
- To report suspected neglect or exploitation of a child, elder, or resident of a long term care facility
- To report births
- To report deaths
- To report specific diseases as required by public health laws
- To report treatment of patients with a physical injury that was inflicted by non-accidental means, such as a stabbing or gunshot wound

Risk Management

The goal of risk management is to reduce adverse events, decrease malpractice claims, and minimize financial loss. It can be proactive (to prevent adverse occurrences) or reactive (damage control). In both cases the risk management process includes:

- Identifying risk or potential risk
- Calculating the probability of an adverse effect from the risk
- Estimating the impact of the adverse effect
- Control of the risk

One of the most widely used retrospective methods to improving safety is the Root Cause Analysis (RCA). RCA is a tool designed to identify what, how, and why an adverse event occurred by identifying the factors that contributed to the undesired outcome. An RCA avoids focusing on mistakes by individuals and instead focuses on errors in the system. Human error is considered inevitable, but management systems can decrease or prevent the likelihood of the adverse event occurring.

There are four steps to the RCA:

1. Data collection and reconstruction of the event in question through review of records and participant interview.

2. Causal factor charting, where information gathered is organized and analyzed by a multidisciplinary team to identify how and why the event occurred. There is rarely one causal factor, so the team should continue analyzing the information until all factors leading to the adverse outcome are identified.

3. Root cause identification, wherein the underlying reason or reasons for the causal factors in Step 2 are identified, so the problems surrounding the occurrence can be addressed.

4. Recommendation and implementation for preventing recurrence.

Legal and Regulatory Requirements

Case managers are at risk for malpractice lawsuits, even though they do not provide direct patient care. Patients most frequently file malpractice claims when they feel the provider was discourteous and did not take time to listen or explain the care to them. Thus, it often comes down to the basics of communication. When a patient feels the provider has listened to him, understands his situation, and has been respectful of his needs, he is very unlikely to seek legal action.

A malpractice lawsuit can arise from an act of omission (that is, failure to do something that should be done) or an act of commission (doing something that should not be done). Either of these is a breach of obligation. The plaintiff, the person bringing forth the malpractice claim, has the burden of proving two points: that the case manager was negligent and that injury resulted from the negligence.

A case manager can take several steps to reduce the risk of a malpractice lawsuit:

- Use only credentialed healthcare providers
- Offer the patient several choices for providers
- Communicate with the patient and address concerns
- Document all communications with the patient and others involved in care and decision-making
- Do not alter records
- Use written guidelines when available; if deviating from them, document justification
- Document compliance or lack of compliance with treatment plan
- Be aware of and comply with professional standards and regulations

Informed Consent

Unlike malpractice law, under tort law a medical professional can be liable if he or she does not obtain informed consent before treating the patient, even if there is no injury or the patient is benefited. For example, if consent is obtained for surgery on the right eye and the surgeon performs surgery on the left eye while the patient is under anesthesia, medical battery has occurred. The surgeon can be held liable even if the patient benefited from the surgery. Other torts include negligence, false imprisonment, and assault.

The following criteria must be met for consent to be informed:

- It must include a discussion of possible side effects, risks, consequences, and benefits of treatment, medication, or procedures, including consequences or risks of stoppage of the service
- The client must have the capacity to make clear, competent decisions

- Consent must be self-determined; that is, it cannot be coerced or pressured by the agency or provider of services
- Information must be clear and easy to understand
- Information must be given verbally and in writing
- The patient must have an opportunity for questions and answers

Interstate Compact for Nursing

Nurse case managers must be licensed in the state where case management is being provided. Telephonic case managers who manage cases across state lines must be licensed in the state where the client is located.

The Nurse Licensure Compact gives nurses the ability to practice nursing across state lines. The nurse must be licensed in his or her state of residency. If the state of residency participates in the compact, he or she can practice in any other compact state.

Negligent Referral

Referral of a patient to a healthcare provider who is known to be unqualified is called negligent referral. The case manager can be held liable for a negligent referral even if he or she is unaware that the provider is unqualified. A reasonably prudent case manager is expected to make sure the referred provider is professionally qualified and without physical or mental impairment that could result in harm to the patient.

Principal/Agent Relationship

A Principal/Agent Relationship is a relationship between a person (aka agent) and another person or entity (aka principal). The agent is authorized to act for the principal. In a healthcare setting, a doctor is an agent employed by the hospital (the principal). The doctor is authorized to act and make decisions on behalf of the hospital for patients, but the principal is responsible for the acts of the agent.

Living Will

A living will specifies which life-sustaining procedures should be performed or withheld if death from a terminal condition is imminent, or if the client is in a permanent vegetative state.

Healthcare Durable Power of Attorney

This document appoints someone to make healthcare decisions on behalf of the client if the client is unable to make decisions for himself.

Healthcare and Disability Related Legislation

The Americans with Disabilities Act

The Americans with Disabilities Act, or ADA, defines an individual with a disability as a person who: 1) has a physical or mental impairment that substantially limits a major life activity, 2) has a record or history of a substantially limiting impairment, or 3) is regarded or perceived by an employer as having a substantially limiting impairment.

The ADA also protects qualified individuals with a prior drug addiction if they have been rehabilitated. However, the ADA provides that the term "individual with a disability" does not include an individual who is currently engaging in the illegal use of drugs.

Assessments are done case by case to determine if the impairment is protected under ADA. An individual, not his or her disability, is protected under ADA.

The ADA prohibits discrimination against people with disabilities in employment, transportation, public accommodation, communications, and governmental activities.

Employers with 15 or more employees are prohibited from discriminating against people with disabilities by Title I of the ADA. In general, the employment provisions of the ADA require:

- Equal opportunity in selecting, testing, and hiring qualified applicants with disabilities
- Job accommodation for applicants and workers with disabilities when such accommodations would not impose "undue hardship" on the employer
- Equal opportunity in promotion and benefits

An applicant with a disability, like all other applicants, must be able to meet the employer's requirements for the job, such as education, training, employment experience, skills, or licenses. In addition, an applicant with a disability must be able to perform the "essential functions" of the job either on his or her own or with the help of "reasonable accommodation."

A job accommodation is a reasonable adjustment to a job or work environment that makes it possible for an individual with a disability to perform job duties. Determining whether to provide accommodations involves considering the required job tasks and the functional limitations of the person doing the job. An employer does not have to provide an accommodation that will cause "undue hardship," defined as being significantly difficult or expensive for the employer. Accommodations may include specialized equipment (such as Dragon dictation or an elevated desk to fit a wheelchair), facility modifications (wheelchair ramps), and adjustments to work schedules or job duties, as well as a range of other creative solutions. The Job Accommodation Network (JAN) provides free consulting on workplace accommodations.

During the application/interview process, the ADA prohibits asking questions such as:

- Do you have a heart condition?
- Do you have asthma or any other difficulties breathing?
- Do you have a disability that would interfere with your ability to perform the job?

- How many days were you sick last year?
- Have you ever filed for workers' compensation? Have you ever been injured on the job?
- Have you ever been treated for mental health problems?
- What prescription drugs are you currently taking?

An employer can ask all of the questions listed above, and others that are likely to reveal the existence of a disability, after it extends a job offer as long as it asks the same questions of other applicants offered the same type of job. In other words, an employer cannot ask such questions only of those who have obvious disabilities. Similarly, an employer may require a medical examination and/or drug screen after making a job offer as long as it requires the same medical examination and/or drug screen of all applicants offered the same type of job. The employer can withdraw the job offer only if it can show that the potential employee is unable to perform the essential functions of the job (with or without reasonable accommodation), or that he poses a significant risk of causing substantial harm to himself or others.

The terms impairment, disability, and handicap are often used interchangeably, but they have very different meanings. Knowing the difference is important. Impairment refers to a problem with a structure or organ of the body. Disability is a functional limitation with regard to a particular activity. Handicap refers to a disadvantage in filling a role in life relative to peers.

Take, for example, a patient who is unable to walk after a spinal cord injury. The impairment is the inability to move his legs. The disability is the inability to walk, and the handicap is that it keeps him from fulfilling his normal role at home, work, and in the community.

Health Insurance Portability and Accountability Act (HIPAA)

HIPAA is the Health Insurance Portability and Accountability Act of 1996. Title I of the Act guarantees health insurance access, portability, and renewal; eliminates some preexisting conditions clauses; and prohibits discrimination based on health status.

Title II of HIPAA creates fraud and abuse controls, the rules for protecting the confidentiality and integrity of a client's health information, and administrative simplification. Most familiar to case managers is the safeguarding of protected health information (PHI). HIPAA covers PHI released, transferred, or divulged outside the agency. According to HIPAA, an authorization for PHI must be in plain, understandable language and contain a detailed description of the information to be released, the purpose of the disclosure, the individual's right to revoke the authorization, and the expiration date of the authorization. HIPAA compliance is required when using fax, phone, and Internet communications. The Act covers not only formal records, but also personal notes and billing information.

Information released under HIPAA becomes protected under the confidentiality guidelines of the organization receiving the information. The agency must have a privacy officer and safeguards to protect client records. The safeguards include electronic security of files (such as passwords) and security of work areas and destruction of files/information.

It is important to note that HIPAA does not apply to disability, auto, liability, or workers' compensation insurance and that state laws take precedence over HIPAA if they are stricter in protecting the privacy of medical records.

Occupational Safety and Health Administration (OSHA) Regulations

OSHA's mission is to assure safe and healthful workplaces by setting and enforcing standards and by providing training, outreach, education, and assistance. Employers are also required to keep their workplaces free of serious recognized hazards.

OSHA standards describe the method that employers must use to protect their employees from hazards. OSHA standards cover construction work, agriculture, maritime operations, and general industry. These standards limit the amount of hazardous chemicals workers can be exposed to, require the use of certain safe practices and equipment, and require employers to monitor hazards and keep records of workplace injuries and illnesses. Examples of OSHA standards include: to provide fall protection, prevent some infections diseases, prevent exposure to harmful substances like asbestos, and provide training for certain dangerous jobs. A General Duty Clause also requires employers to keep the workplace free of serious recognized hazards.

OSHA covers private sector workers, not government employees. State and local government workers may be covered by an OSHA-approved state program, and federal agencies must have a safety and health program that meets the same standards as private employers. OSHA does not penalize federal agencies, but it does monitor them and respond to workers' complaints.

Family Medical Leave Act (FMLA)

The Family and Medical Leave Act (FMLA) provides eligible employees up to 12 workweeks of unpaid leave a year for specified family and medical reasons. It requires group health benefits be maintained during the leave, as if the employee continued to work. Employees are also entitled to return to their same or an equivalent job at the end of their FMLA leave.

Eligible employees are those who:
- Work for a covered employer (public agencies, including government and local schools, as well as private sector employees working for companies with 50 or more employees)
- Have worked 1,250 hours during the 12 months prior to the start of leave
- Have worked for the employer for 12 months

FMLA may be taken for:

- Birth, adoption, or foster care of a child
- Care of spouse, child, or parent who has a serious health condition
- A serious health condition that makes the employee unable to perform the essential functions of his or her job

FMLA does not have to be taken all at once; it can be taken intermittently—taking leave in blocks of time for a single qualifying reason—or to reduce the employee's daily or weekly work schedule. FMLA works on a rolling year, not a calendar year. The first day leave is taken begins the year.

The FMLA only requires that employers provide unpaid leave. However, the law permits an employee to elect, or the employer to require, that the employee use accrued paid vacation leave or paid sick or family leave for some or all of the FMLA leave period. An employee must follow the employer's normal leave rules in order to substitute paid leave. When paid leave is used for an FMLA-covered reason, the leave is FMLA-protected. If the leave is unpaid, the employee must continue to pay his portion of the medical insurance that was normally deducted from his paycheck.

Mental Health Parity Act of 1996

The Mental Health Parity Act does not mandate mental health benefits be offered in health insurance plans. However, it does require that when this benefit is provided, the lifetime or annual dollar limits on mental health care must be the same as the limits that apply to medical or surgical benefits. Substance abuse and chemical dependency are not covered under this act.

Pregnancy Discrimination Act

The Pregnancy Discrimination Act:

- Forbids discrimination based on pregnancy in any aspect of employment, including hiring, firing, pay, job assignments, leave, and health insurance

- Requires health insurance provided by the employer to cover expenses for pregnancy-related conditions on the same basis as costs for other medical conditions
- Ensures employees on leave due to pregnancy-related conditions are treated the same as other temporarily disabled employees

Newborns' and Mothers' Health Protection Act of 1996

The Newborns' and Mothers' Health Protection Act requires that health plans and insurance issuers not restrict a mother's or newborn's benefits for a hospital stay connected to childbirth to less than 48 hours following a vaginal delivery or 96 hours following a delivery by cesarean section. However, the attending provider (who may be a physician or nurse midwife) may decide, after consulting with the mother, to discharge the mother or newborn child earlier. Incentives (either positive or negative) that could encourage an attending provider to give less than the minimum protections under the Act as described above are prohibited.

Women's Health and Cancer Rights Act of 1998

The Act requires that group health plans providing coverage for mastectomies also cover the following:

- Reconstruction of the breast that was removed by mastectomy
- Surgery and reconstruction of the other breast to make the breasts appear symmetrical
- Breast prostheses
- Complications at all stages of mastectomy, including lymphedema

Affordable Care Act (ACA)

The Affordable Care Act (ACA) has created comprehensive health insurance reforms designed to improve access, affordability, and quality in healthcare. Since its signing on March 23, 2010, the law was gradually phased in over five years and is now in full effect. The following is an overview of the key aspects of the law.

End to pre-existing condition discrimination

Insurance companies can no longer deny coverage or charge more because of a pre-existing condition. They also cannot charge more based on gender. Once insured the insurance company cannot refuse to cover treatment for pre-existing conditions. The one exception to this is grandfathered individual health insurance policies bought on or before March 23, 2010.

End to arbitrary withdrawals of insurance coverage

Insurance companies can no longer drop coverage due to an honest mistake made on the application. The insurance company can rescind coverage if the application is intentionally falsified or if premium payments are not made on time, but it must give at least 30 days' notice to allow time to appeal the decision or find new coverage.

Keeps young adults covered

Adult children who cannot get coverage through their jobs may remain on their parents' policies until they are 26.

Free preventative care benefits

Insurers are now required to cover a number of recommended preventive services without additional cost sharing such as copays or deductibles. Depending on age, these preventive services include:
- Blood pressure, diabetes, and cholesterol testing
- Some cancer screenings, including mammograms and colonoscopies
- Counseling on topics such as smoking cessation, weight loss, healthy eating, treating depression, and reducing alcohol use
- Well-baby and well-child visits from birth to age 21

- Routine vaccinations
- Counseling, screening, and vaccines to ensure healthy pregnancies
- Flu and pneumonia shots

It is important to note that grandfathered plans may not provide these preventive benefits for free. Also, the health plan can require the use of network providers to receive these benefits without cost sharing. Finally, there may still be a fee for the office visit related to these services.

Coverage of essential health benefits

All plans offered in the individual and small group markets must cover a comprehensive package of items and services known as essential health benefits. In addition, states expanding their Medicaid programs must provide these benefits to people newly eligible for Medicaid.

Essential health benefits must include items and services within at least the following 10 categories:

- Ambulatory patient services
- Emergency services
- Hospitalization
- Maternity and newborn care
- Mental health and substance use disorder services, including behavioral health treatment (this includes counseling and psychotherapy)
- Prescription drugs
- Rehabilitative and habilitative services and devices
- Laboratory services
- Preventive and wellness services and chronic disease management
- Pediatric services, including oral and vision care (but adult dental and vision coverage are not essential health benefits)

These essential health benefits are subject to deductibles and copays. In addition, self-funded employer plans and grandfathered plans are not required to cover these benefits.

End to dollar limits on care

The ACA bans annual and lifetime dollar limits on most covered health benefits. In the past, people with cancer or other illnesses could lose their insurance coverage when their healthcare expenses reached the dollar limit on their policy. There are some exceptions to this ban on limits—for example, grandfathered individual plans are not required to follow the rules on annual limits—and plans can put an annual dollar limit and a lifetime dollar limit on spending for healthcare services that are not essential health benefits.

Ensuring coverage for individuals participating in clinical trials

Insurers are prohibited from dropping or limiting coverage because an individual chooses to participate in a clinical trial. This applies to all clinical trials that treat cancer or other life-threatening diseases.

Closing the Medicare donut hole

Most Medicare Prescription Drug Plans have a coverage gap known as a "the donut hole." This refers to a point in coverage when the participant and drug plan have spent a specified dollar amount, and the participant must pay out of pocket for his prescriptions until another dollar amount is reached. The ACA gives participants in the donut hole a discount on drugs. This discount is applied automatically at the pharmacy and increases each year until the ACA closes the donut hole completely in 2020. From that point on, participants will only pay usual drug copays.

Guaranteed right to appeal

Under the ACA the participant has the right to appeal a health insurance company's decision to deny payment for a claim or to terminate health coverage.

The participant will first request an internal appeal. If the insurance company upholds its decision to deny payment or coverage, the law permits the participant to request an external review. In an external review, an independent third party decides whether to uphold or overturn the insurance company's decision.

Expands the Mental Health Parity and Addiction Equality Act (MHPAEA) of 2008

The MHPAEA does not require the coverage of mental health or substance use treatment. It does, however, require group health plans and insurers that cover mental health and substance use treatment to provide the same level of coverage that they do for general medical and surgical care. This applies to:

- Copays, coinsurance, deductibles, and out-of-pocket maximums
- Limitations on service utilization, such as limits on the number of inpatient days or outpatient visits covered
- Coverage for out-of-network providers

The ACA further expands the MHPAEA by requiring the coverage of:

- Behavioral health treatment, such as psychotherapy and counseling
- Mental and behavioral health inpatient services
- Substance use disorder treatment
- Alcohol misuse screening and counseling
- Depression screening
- Tobacco use screening and cessation interventions
- Domestic and interpersonal violence screening and counseling
- Behavioral assessment for children

Creates a health insurance marketplace

State health exchanges were devised to organize the health insurance marketplace so consumers and small businesses could more easily access and purchase healthcare coverage based on price, coverage features, benefits, and services. It was also designed to place individuals and small businesses on more equal ground with large group plans through pooling of risk, market leverage, and economies of scale.

Reducing paperwork and administrative costs

The ACA instituted changes to standardize billing and required health plans to implement rules for the secure and confidential electronic exchange of health information.

Paying physicians based on value not volume

A provision that took effect in 2015 ties physician Medicare payments to the quality of care they provide. Medicare payments will be modified so that physicians who provide higher value care will receive higher payments than those who provide lower quality care.

Linking payment to quality outcomes

The law established a hospital Value-Based Purchasing program (VBP) in traditional Medicare. This program offers financial incentives to hospitals to improve the quality of care. It is based on either: 1) how well they perform on each measure compared to other hospitals, or 2) how much they improved their own performance on each measure compared to their performance during a prior baseline period. Hospital performance is required to be publicly reported, beginning with measures relating to heart attacks, heart failure, pneumonia, surgical care, health-care associated infections, and patients' perception of care.

Hospital Readmission Reduction Program

The ACA authorizes Medicare to reduce payments to acute care hospitals with excess readmissions that are paid under CMS's Inpatient Prospective Payment System (IPPS). Excess readmissions are measured by a ratio, by dividing a hospital's number of "predicted" 30-day readmissions for heart attack, heart failure, pneumonia, hip/knee replacement, and COPD, by the number that would be "expected," based on an average hospital with similar patients. A ratio greater than 1 indicates excess readmissions.

The ACA also identifies ways to improve the often-fragmented healthcare system, such as the patient-centered medical home and the accountable care organization. Both of these rely on care coordination as a central pillar of their success.

More information on these models of care can be found in the chapter Delivery and Reimbursement Methods under Models of Care.

Impact for Case Management

The ACA provides many incentives to improve quality, coordinate care, and decrease costs—all areas where case managers are well positioned to take the lead. The impact case managers can have in this new value-driven care world are tremendous. Case management functions, such as assessing, planning, educating, discharge planning, care transitioning, care coordination, and monitoring, are key to meeting the savings benchmarks and quality performance standards outlined in the ACA.

Meaningful Use

Meaningful Use is a CMS program that awards incentives for using certified electronic health records (EHRs) to:

- Improve quality, safety, and efficiency, and reduce health disparities
- Engage patients and families
- Improve care coordination and public health
- Maintain privacy and security of patient health information

The goal of Meaningful Use is better clinical outcomes, improved population health outcomes, increased transparency and efficiency, empowered individuals, and more robust research data on health systems.

The American Recovery and Reinvestment Act of 2009 stipulates the following three components of Meaningful Use:

- The use of certified EHR in a meaningful manner (e.g., e-prescribing)
- The use of certified EHR technology for electronic exchange of health information to improve the quality of healthcare
- The use of certified EHR technology to submit clinical quality measures and other measures

Meaningful Use sets specific objectives that eligible professionals (EPs) and hospitals must achieve to qualify for Medicare and Medicaid EHR Incentive Programs. The following is a closer look at a few of the objectives and their clinical importance.

Electronic Exchanges of Summary of Care

Objective

EPs who transition their patients to another setting of care or provider of care, or refer their patients to another provider of care, should provide a summary care record for each transition of care or referral. For this objective, the term "transition of care" is defined as the movement of a patient from one setting of care (e.g., hospital, ambulatory primary care practice, specialty care practice, long-term care, home health care, or rehabilitation facility) to another. A summary of care record must include the following elements:

- Patient name
- Referring or transitioning provider's name and office contact information
- Procedures
- Encounter diagnosis

- Immunizations
- Laboratory test results
- Vital signs (height, weight, blood pressure, BMI)
- Smoking status
- Functional status, including activities of daily living, cognitive and disability status
- Demographic information (preferred language, sex, race, ethnicity, date of birth)
- Care plan field (at a minimum the following components must be included: problem-focus of the care plan, goal-target outcome, and any instructions that the provider has given to the patient)
- Care team, including the primary care provider of record and any additional known care team members beyond the referring or transitioning provider and the receiving provider
- Reason for the referral
- Current problem list (at minimum a list of current, active, and historical diagnoses, but the problem list is not limited to diagnoses)
- Current medication list
- Current medication allergy list

Clinical importance

A transition of care summary, also known as a discharge summary in some circumstances, provides essential clinical information for the receiving care team and helps organize final clinical and administrative activities for the transferring care team. This summary helps ensure the coordination and continuity of healthcare as patients transfer between different locations or different levels of care within the same location. This document improves transitions and discharges, communication among providers, and cross-setting relationships, which can improve care quality and safety.

Reporting Specific Cases

Objective

To identify and report specific cases to a specialized registry (other than a cancer registry), except where prohibited, and in accordance with applicable law and practice. For this objective, the term "Specialized Registry" is defined as those sponsored by the national specialty societies as well as specialized registries maintained by public health agencies.

Clinical importance

Reporting to registries can assist in gathering public health information. These registries can assist providers in evaluating the health status of their patients, facilitate interventions for prevention and screening, and provide access to public health agencies to better care for and improve the population's health.

Reporting Cancer Cases

Objective

To identify and report cancer cases to a public health central cancer registry, except where prohibited, and in accordance with applicable law and practice.

Clinical importance

Reporting to cancer registries can remedy the underreporting of cancer cases, primarily in the outpatient setting. Facilitating electronic reporting either automatically or upon verification by providers can address this barrier by identifying reportable cancer cases and treatments. This information can be used to identify population trends, such as the identification of underlying risk factors or treatments that may influence quality of life or survival.

Structured Electronic Transmission of Laboratory Test Results

Objective

To incorporate clinical lab-test results into Certified EHR Technology (CEHRT) as structured data.

Clinical importance

Incomplete or misplaced test results make efficient, safe, and effective clinical decision-making difficult. Lab and test results placed directly in the patient's record allows for ease of access and reference when and where it is needed. The availability of structured lab results within the EHR contributes to office efficiencies while also assisting providers make real time decisions about patient care.

E-Prescribing (eRx)

Objective

To generate and transmit permissible prescriptions electronically.

Definitions of terms:

> Permissible Prescriptions – Refers to the current restrictions established by the Department of Justice on electronic prescribing for controlled substances in Schedule II-V. Any prescription not subject to these restrictions would be permissible.

> Prescription – The authorization by an EP to a pharmacist to dispense a drug that the pharmacist would not dispense to the patient without such authorization.

Clinical importance

Electronic prescribing is a fast, efficient way to write/reorder and transmit prescriptions. eRx has pre-set fields, so all required information is entered and automatically stored in the patient's record for easy review during follow-up visits or for transitions to other providers. e-Prescribing increases overall patient satisfaction because the prescriptions can be automatically transmitted to a pharmacy of preference. Electronic systems also provide guided dose algorithms to assist providers. Providers may also query the patient's health plan formulary to ensure the drug selected is covered, which may reduce costs to the patient.

Clinical Pathways, Standards of Care, and Practice Guidelines

Evidence-based Practice Guidelines and Treatment Guidelines

Evidence-based practice is the process of applying the best available research when making decisions about healthcare. Numerous professionals analyze new research information and develop practice guidelines. The guidelines give the provider and the patient recommendations for screening, diagnostic workup, and treatment that are believed to provide the best outcome.

These guidelines are not meant to replace the clinical judgment of the individual provider or establish a standard of care. They are meant to be flexible and are only considered recommendations. Healthcare professionals who promote evidence-based guidelines use research evidence along with clinical expertise and patient preferences in providing care.

Treatment guidelines are similar to practice guidelines but focus on assisting providers in deciding on the most appropriate treatment for clinical conditions. Like practice guidelines, treatment guidelines are recommendations, not standards of care.

Standards of Care

Whereas guidelines are meant to be flexible, standards are a rigid set of criteria meant to be followed under any circumstances. These practices are medically necessary for the management of a clinical condition.

Clinical Pathway

A clinical pathway provides outcome-focused care within a certain timeline. Clinical pathways develop algorithms from evidence-based guidelines, standards of care, and protocols for common diagnoses, conditions, and procedures. These algorithms are used by a multidisciplinary care team in providing care to the patient. Clinical pathways standardize treatments, promote efficiency, and improve the continuity and coordination of care provided by all disciplines involved. This results in greater quality of care and decreased costs.

Items addressed on the clinical pathway may include:

- Patient assessment and monitoring
- Tests and procedures
- Treatments
- Consultations
- Medications
- Activity
- Nutrition
- Education
- Targeted length of stay
- Outcome criteria
- Notification for deviations

Self-care and Well-being as a Professional

In the course of their work, case managers are routinely confronted with challenging patients and circumstances. They are in contact with multiple "clients," including patients, their families, physicians, employers, insurance companies, and vendors, all of whom may have their own agendas and priorities. Often case managers are asked to do more with less, which can add to the stress and overwhelm of their job. It is common that, in the course of caring for everyone else, they neglect caring for themselves.

Case managers should actively look after their own well-being so they can effectively support their clients. Although self-care is a personal matter that everyone approaches differently, there are some fundamental components, such as lowering stress, engaging in healthy practices, and participating in activities that give energy. Ways to engage in self-care include:

- Exercising regularly
- Eating a well balanced diet
- Developing a regular sleep routine and getting adequate sleep
- Engaging in hobbies or interests
- Fostering positive relationships
- Taking breaks throughout the day, including a lunch break
- Learning to say no
- Taking time to relax

Self-care is a daily, long-term activity that takes practice. When case management work gets overwhelming, it's important to keep things in perspective, ask for help, and embrace change.

Additional Resources

Affordable Care Act

Key Features of the Affordable Care Act by Year: http://www.hhs.gov/healthcare/facts-and-features/key-features-of-aca-by-year/index.html#2010

Substance Abuse and Mental Health Services Administration: http://www.samhsa.gov/health-financing/implementation-mental-health-parity-addiction-equity-act

Mental Health and Substance Abuse Coverage: https://www.healthcare.gov/coverage/mental-health-substance-abuse-coverage/

Affordable Care Act: http://www.hhs.gov/healthcare/

Affordable Care Act: https://www.healthcare.gov/coverage/what-marketplace-plans-cover/

Affordable Care Act: https://aspe.hhs.gov/report/affordable-care-act-expands-mental-health-and-substance-use-disorder-benefits-and-federal-parity-protections-62-million-americans

Medicare, Linking Quality to Payment: https://www.medicare.gov/hospitalcompare/linking-quality-to-payment.html

Ethics Related to Care Delivery and Professional Practice

CCMC Ethics Requirements for Renewal: https://ccmcertification.org/center-stage/ce-update-ethics-related-ce-required-ccm-renewal

Case Management Society of America: http://www.cmsa.org/

CCMC Code of Professional Conduct for Case Managers: https://ccmcertification.org/about-us/about-case-management/guidelines-practice

Glossary

The following terms are a selection of the CCMC's Glossary of Terms available on their website at: https://ccmcertification.org/sites/default/files/downloads/2011/CCMC%20Glossary.pdf

Accreditation: A standardized program for evaluating healthcare organizations to ensure a specified level of quality, as defined by a set of national industry standards. Organizations that meet accreditation standards receive an official authorization or approval of their services. Accreditation entails a voluntary survey process that assesses the extent of a healthcare organization's compliance with the standards. The purpose is to improve the systems and processes of care and, in so doing, improving patient outcomes.

Acuity: A way to measure complexity and severity of a patient's health/medical condition.

Administrative Services Only (ASO): An insurance company or third party administrator (TPA) that provides administrative services for an employer group. The employer is usually self-insured or at-risk for the cost of healthcare services provided, and the ASO processes and manages the claims.

Advance Directive: Legally executed document that explains the patient's healthcare-related wishes and decisions. It is prepared while the patient is competent and is used if the patient becomes incapacitated or incompetent to make healthcare decisions for himself.

Adverse Events: Any untoward occurrences that are not natural consequences of the patient's disease process or treatment outcomes under most conditions.

Advocacy: Acting on behalf of those who are not able to speak for or represent themselves. It also includes defending others and acting in their best interest. A person or group involved in such activities is called an advocate.

Algorithm: The chronological delineation of the steps in, or activities of, patient care, as they relate to specific conditions/situations.

Alternate Level of Care: A level of care that can safely be used in place of the current level; it is determined based on the acuity and complexity of the patient's condition and the type of needed services and resources.

Ambulatory Payment Classification (APC) System: An encounter-based classification system for outpatient reimbursement, including hospital-based clinics, emergency departments, observation, and ambulatory surgery. Payment rates are based on categories of services that are similar in cost and resource utilization.

Ancillary Services: Other diagnostic and therapeutic services that may be involved in the care of patients other than nursing or medicine. Includes respiratory, laboratory, radiology, nutrition, physical and occupational therapy, and pastoral services.

Appeal: The formal process or request to reconsider a decision to deny admission for healthcare services, reimbursement for services rendered, or a patient's request for extending the length of stay.

Appropriateness of Settings: Used to determine if the level of care needed is being delivered in the most appropriate and cost-effective setting possible.

Approved Charge: The amount insurance pays a physician based on the Medicare fee schedule. Physicians may bill the beneficiaries for an additional amount, subject to the limiting care allowed.

Assessment: The process of collecting in-depth information about a person's situation and functioning to identify individual needs. It is used to develop a comprehensive case management plan that will address those needs. In addition to direct client contact, information should be gathered from other relevant sources (such as professional caregivers, non-professional caregivers, employers, health records, educational/military records, etc.).

Assistive Device: Any tool that is designed, made, or adapted to assist a person to perform a particular task.

Assistive Technology: Any item, piece of equipment, or product system, whether acquired commercially or off the shelf, modified, or customized, that is used to increase, maintain, or improve functional capabilities of individuals with disabilities. Examples are listening devices, speech production equipment, and low vision devices.

Assistive Technology Services: Any service that directly assists an individual with a disability in the selection, acquisition, or use of an assistive technology device.

Autonomy: A form of personal liberty in which the patient holds the right and freedom to select and initiate his or her own treatment and course of action. The patient takes control of his or her health. It entails fostering the patient's independence and self-determination.

Beneficence: The obligation and duty to promote good, to further and support a patient's legitimate interests and decisions, and to actively prevent or remove harm. To share with the patient risks associated with a particular treatment option.

Beneficiary: An individual eligible for benefits under a particular plan. Beneficiaries may be known as "members" in HMO plans or "enrollees" in PPO plans. Also a common term for people who are covered by Medicare.

Benefit Package: The sum of services a health plan, government agency, or employer contracts to provide. In addition to basic physician and hospital services, some plans also cover prescriptions, dental, and vision care.

Benefits: The amount payable by the insurance company to a claimant or beneficiary under the claimant's specific coverage.

Brain Disorder: A loosely-used term for a neurological disorder or syndrome indicating impairment or injury to brain tissue.

Brain Injury: Any damage to tissues of the brain that leads to impairment of the function of the Central Nervous System.

Burden of Proof: The duty of producing evidence as a legal case progresses, and/or the duty to establish the truth of the claim by a preponderance of evidence. The former may pass from party to party; the latter rests throughout upon the party asserting the affirmative of the issue.

Capitation: A fixed amount of money per-member-per-month (PMPM) paid to a care provider for covered services rather than based on specific services provided. It is the typical reimbursement method used by HMOs. Whether a member uses the health service once or more than once, a capitated provider receives the same payment.

Caregiver: The person responsible for caring for a patient in the home setting. Can be a family member, friend, volunteer, or an assigned healthcare professional.

CARF: Commission on Accreditation of Rehabilitation Facilities. A private, non-profit organization that establishes standards of quality for services to people with disabilities. It offers voluntary accreditation for rehabilitation facilities based on a set of nationally recognized standards.

Carve Out: Services that are excluded from a provider contract (but that may be covered through arrangements with other providers). Providers are not financially responsible for services carved out of their contract.

Caseload: The total number of patients followed by a case manager at any point in time.

Case Management: A collaborative process that assesses, plans, implements, coordinates, monitors, and evaluates the options and services required to meet an individual's health needs, using communication and available resources to promote quality, cost-effective outcomes.

Case Management Plan: A timeline of patient care activities and expected outcomes that address the plan of care for each discipline involved with a particular patient. It is usually developed prospectively by an interdisciplinary healthcare team in relation to a patient's diagnosis, health problem, or surgical procedure.

Case Mix Group (CMG): A CMG determines the base payment rate for inpatient rehabilitation facilities under the Medicare system.

Case Mix Index (CMI): The sum of the DRG-relative weights of all patients/cases seen during a one-year period in an organization, divided by the number of patients hospitalized and treated during the same year.

Case Rates: Rate of reimbursement that packages pricing for a certain category of services. Typically combines facility and professional practitioner fees for care and services.

Catastrophic Case: Any medical condition or illness that has heightened medical, social, and financial consequences that responds positively to the control offered through a systematic effort of case management.

Claim: A request for payment of reparation for a loss covered by an insurance contract.

Clinical Pathway/Case Management Plan: A timeline of patient care activities and expected outcomes of care. It addresses the plan of care of each discipline involved in the care of a particular patient. It is usually developed prospectively by an interdisciplinary healthcare team in relation to a patient's diagnosis, health problem, or surgical procedure.

Coding: A mechanism of identifying and defining patient care services/activities as primary and secondary diagnoses and procedures. The process is guided by the International Classification of Disease coding manual (i.e., the ICD-10), which lists the various codes and their respective descriptions. Coding is usually done in preparation for reimbursement for services provided.

Cognitive Rehabilitation: Therapy programs that aid persons in managing specific problems in perception, memory, thinking, and problem-solving. Practices and strategies are taught to help improve function and/or compensate for remaining deficits.

Coinsurance: A type of cost sharing in which the insured person pays or shares part of the medical bill, usually according to a fixed percentage.

Communication Skills: Refers to the many ways of transferring thought from one person to another though the commonly used media of speech, written words, or bodily gestures.

Community-based Programs: Support programs that are located in a community environment as opposed to an institutional setting.

Comorbidity: A preexisting condition (usually chronic) that, because of its presence with a specific condition, causes an increase in the length of stay by about one day in 75% of patients.

Competence: The mental ability and capacity to make decisions, accomplish actions, and perform tasks that another person of similar background and training, or any human being, would be reasonably expected to perform adequately.

Concurrent Review: A method of reviewing patient care and services during a hospital stay to validate the necessity of care and to explore alternatives to inpatient care. It is also a form of utilization review that tracks the consumption of resources and the progress of patients while being treated.

Confidential Communications: Certain classes of communications that the law will not permit to be divulged. For example, communications passed between persons in confidential or fiduciary relations to each other (or who, on account of their relative situation, are under a special duty of secrecy and fidelity).

Consensus: Agreement in opinion of experts. Building consensus is a method for developing case management plans.

Continued Stay Review: A type of review used to determine whether each day of the hospital stay is necessary and that care is being rendered at the appropriate level. It takes place during a patient's hospitalization.

Continuous Quality Improvement (CQI): A key component of total quality management that uses rigorous, systematic, organization-wide processes to achieve ongoing improvement in the quality of healthcare services and operations. It focuses on both outcomes and processes of care.

Continuum of Care: The continuum of care matches ongoing needs of the individuals being served by the case management process with the appropriate level and type of health, medical, financial, legal, and psychosocial care. Health services are within a setting or across multiple settings.

Coordination: The process of organizing, securing, integrating, and modifying the resources necessary to accomplish the goals set forth in the case management plan.

Coordination of Benefits (COB): An agreement that prevents double payment for services when a subscriber has coverage from two or more sources. It uses language developed by the National Association of Insurance Commissioners.

Copayment: A supplemental cost-sharing arrangement between the member and the insurer in which the member pays a specific charge for a specified service. Copayments may be flat or variable amounts per unit of service and may be for such things as physician office visits, prescriptions, or hospital services. The payment is incurred at the time of service.

Credentialing: A review process to approve a provider who applies to participate in a health plan. Specific criteria are applied to evaluate participation in the plan. The review may include references, training, experience, demonstrated ability, licensure verification, and adequate malpractice insurance.

Cultural Competency: A set of congruent behaviors, attitudes, and policies that come together in a system, agency, or among professionals and enables that system, agency, or those professionals to work effectively in cross-cultural situations.

Culture: The thoughts, communications, actions, customs, beliefs, values, and institutions of racial, ethnic, religious, or social groups.

Current Procedural Terminology (CPT): A listing of descriptive terms and identifying codes for reporting medical services and procedures performed by healthcare providers. It is usually used for billing purposes.

Custodial Care: Care provided primarily to assist a patient in meeting the activities of daily living but not requiring skilled nursing care.

Database: An organized, comprehensive collection of patient care data. May be used for research or for quality improvement efforts.

Deductible: Under a medical insurance plan, a specific amount of money the insured person must pay before the insurer's payments for covered healthcare services begin.

Denial: When no authorization or certification is given by the insurance company for healthcare services because of the inability to provide justification of medical necessity or appropriateness of treatment or length of stay. This can occur before, during, or after care provision.

Developmental Disability: Any mental and/or physical disability with onset before age 22 and that may continue indefinitely. It can limit major life activities. Individuals with intellectual disability, cerebral palsy, autism, epilepsy and other seizure disorders, sensory impairments, congenital disabilities, traumatic brain injury, or conditions caused by disease (e.g., polio or muscular dystrophy) may be considered developmentally disabled.

Diagnosis-Related Group (DRG): A patient classification scheme that provides a means of relating the type of patient a hospital treats to the cost incurred by the hospital. DRGs group patients according to similar resource consumption and length of stay. It is the method of reimbursement used by CMS to pay hospitals for Medicare and Medicaid recipients. It is used by a few states for all payers and by many private health plans (usually non-HMO) for contracting purposes. DRGs may be primary or secondary; an outlier classification also exists.

Disability:

1) A physical or neurological deviation in an individual makeup. It may refer to a physical, mental, or sensory condition. A disability may or may not be a handicap to an individual, depending on one's adjustment to it.

2) Diminished function, based on the anatomic, physiological, or mental impairment that has reduced an individual's activity or presumed ability to engage in any substantial gainful activity.

3) Inability or limitation in performing tasks, activities, and roles in the manner or within the range considered normal for a person of the same age, gender, culture, and education. It can also refer to any restriction or lack of ability (resulting from an impairment) to perform an activity in the manner or within the range considered normal for a human being.

Disability Income Insurance: A form of health insurance that provides periodic payments to replace income when an insured person is unable to work as a result of illness, injury, or disease.

Eligibility: The determination that an individual has met requirements to obtain benefits under a specific health plan contract.

Employability: Having skills and training commonly necessary to be gainfully employed on a reasonably continuous basis, when considering the person's age, education, experience, physical, and mental capacities due to industrial injury or disease.

Enrollee: An individual subscribed to a health benefit plan provided by a public or private healthcare insurance organization.

Ergonomics: The scientific discipline concerned with the understanding of interactions among humans and other elements of a system. The profession applies theory, principles, data, and methods to environmental design (including work environments) in order to optimize human well-being and overall system performance.

Exclusive Provider Organization (EPO): A managed care plan that provides benefits only if care is rendered by providers within a specific network.

Fee Schedule: A listing of fee allowances that a health plan will pay for specific procedures or services.

Fee-for-Service (FFS): An insurance payment system in which providers are paid for each service performed, in contrast to capitation. Fee schedules are an example of fee-for-service.

Formulary: The prescription drugs covered by a specific health plan. Providers may choose effective medications from this list.

Functional Capacity Evaluation (FCE): A systematic process of assessing an individual's physical capacities and functional abilities. The FCE matches human performance levels to the demands of a specific job, work activity, or occupation. It establishes the physical level of work an individual can perform. The FCE is useful in determining job placement, job accommodation, or return to work after injury or illness. FCEs can provide objective information regarding functional work ability in the determination of occupational disability status.

Functional Job Analysis: Defines the job requirements, including both essential and nonessential duties.

Gatekeeper: A primary care physician (usually a family practitioner, internist, pediatrician, or nurse practitioner) to whom a plan member is assigned. The gatekeeper is responsible for managing all referrals for specialty care and other covered services used by the member.

Global Fee: A predetermined all-inclusive fee for a specific set of related services, treated as a single unit for billing or reimbursement purposes.

Group Model HMO: The HMO contracts with a group of physicians to provide many health services in a central location, for a set fee per patient. The group of physicians determines the compensation of each individual physician, often sharing profits.

Habilitation: The process by which a person with developmental disabilities is assisted in acquiring and maintaining life skills to: 1) cope more effectively with personal and developmental demands, and 2) increase the level of physical, mental, vocational, and social ability through services. Persons with developmental disabilities include anyone whose development has been delayed, interrupted, or stopped/fixed by injury or disease after an initial period of normal development, as well as those with congenital conditions.

Handicap: The functional disadvantage and limitation of potential due to a physical or mental impairment or disability. It substantially limits or prevents the fulfillment of one or more major life activities otherwise considered normal for that individual based on age, sex, and social and cultural factors, such as caring for oneself, performing manual tasks, walking, seeing, hearing, speaking, breathing, learning, working, etc. Handicap is a classification of role reduction resulting from circumstances that place an impaired or disabled person at a disadvantage compared to other persons.

Health and Human Services Risk Management: The science of the identification, evaluation, and treatment of financial (and clinical) loss. A program that attempts to provide positive avoidance of negative results.

Health Insurance: Protection that provides payment of benefits for covered sickness or injury. There are various types of health insurance, such as accident insurance, disability income insurance, medical expense insurance, and accidental death and dismemberment insurance.

Health Maintenance Organization (HMO): An organization that provides or arranges for coverage of designated health services for a fixed prepaid premium. There are four basic models of HMO: group model, individual practice association (IPA), network model, and staff model. Under the Federal HMO Act, an organization must possess the following to call itself an HMO: 1) an organized system for providing healthcare in a geographical area, 2) an agreed-on set of basic and supplemental health maintenance and treatment services, and 3) a voluntarily enrolled group of people.

Healthcare Proxy: A legal document that directs the healthcare provider/agency in whom to contact for approval/consent of treatment decisions or options when the patient is no longer deemed competent to decide for him- or herself.

Home Health Resource Group (HHRG): Groupings for prospective reimbursement under Medicare for home health agencies. Placement into an HHRG is based on the OASIS score (see definition below). Reimbursement rates correspond to the level of home healthcare provided.

Hospice: A system of inpatient and outpatient care that is supportive, palliative, and family-centered, designed to assist a terminally ill individual be comfortable and maintain a satisfactory lifestyle through the end of life.

ICD-10-CM: International Classification of Diseases, Tenth Revision, Clinical Modification. It is formulated to standardize diagnoses and is used for coding medical records in preparation for reimbursement, particularly in the inpatient care setting.

Impairment: A general term indicating injury, deficiency, or lessening of function. Impairment is a condition that is medically determined and relates to the loss or abnormality of psychological, physiological, or anatomical structure or function. Impairments are disturbances at the level of the organ and include defects or loss of limb, organ, or other body structure or mental function (e.g., amputation, paralysis, mental retardation, or psychiatric disturbances).

Implementation: The process of executing specific case management activities and/or interventions that will lead to accomplishing the goals set forth in the case management plan.

Indemnity Benefits: Insurance benefits in the form of payments rather than services. The provider bills the patient for services; the patient is reimbursed by his insurance company.

Indicator: A measure or metric that can be used to monitor and assess quality and outcomes of important aspects of care or services. It measures the performance of functions, processes, and outcomes of an organization.

Individual Practice Association (IPA) Model HMO: An HMO model that contracts with private practice physicians or a healthcare association to provide healthcare services for a negotiated fee. The physicians continue in their existing individual or group practice.

Informed Consent: Consent given by a patient, next of kin, legal guardian, or designated person for an intervention, treatment, or service after the provision of sufficient information by the provider. A decision based on knowledge of the advantages and disadvantages and implications of choosing a particular course of action.

Injury: Any wrong, or damages done to another; may be done to his/her person, rights, reputation, or property.

Inpatient Rehabilitation Facilities Patient Assessment Instrument (IRF-PAI): An instrument that classifies patients into distinct groups based on clinical characteristics and expected resource needs. The PAI determines the Case Mix Group (CMG) classification.

Insurance Risk Management: A comprehensive program of activities to identify, evaluate, and take corrective action against risks; these risks may lead to patient or staff injury with resulting financial loss or legal liability. This program aims at minimizing losses.

Integrated Delivery System (IDS): A single organization or a group of affiliated organizations that provides a wide spectrum of ambulatory and tertiary care and services. Care may also be provided across various settings of the healthcare continuum.

Intensity of Service: An acuity of illness criteria based on the evaluation/treatment plan, interventions, and anticipated outcomes.

Intervention: Planned strategies and activities that modify maladaptive behaviors or states of being and facilitate growth and change. Intervention is analogous to the medical term treatment. Intervention may include activities such as advocacy, psychotherapy, or speech language therapy.

JCAHO: Joint Commission on Accreditation of Health Care Organizations.

Justice: Maintaining what is right and fair and making decisions that are good for the patient.

Length of Stay: The number of days that a health plan member/patient stays in an inpatient, home health, or hospice facility.

Level of Care: The intensity of effort required to diagnose, treat, preserve, or maintain an individual's physical or emotional status.

Levels of Service: Based on the patient's condition and the needed care, used to identify and verify that the patient is receiving care at the appropriate level.

Liability: Legal responsibility for failure to act appropriately or for actions that do not meet the standards of care, inflicting harm on another person.

Life Care Plan: A dynamic document based on published standards of practice, comprehensive assessment, research, and data analysis. For individuals who have chronic healthcare needs or have experienced catastrophic injury, it provides an organized, concise plan for current and future needs alongside associated costs.

Living Will: A legal document that directs the healthcare team/provider in holding or withdrawing life support measures. It is usually prepared by the patient while he or she is competent, indicating the patient's wishes.

Long-Term Disability Income Insurance: Insurance issued to an employee, group, or individual to replace a portion of an individual's earned income if the income is lost as a result of a serious, prolonged illness during the normal work career.

Malpractice: Improper care or treatment by a healthcare professional. A wrongful conduct.

Managed Care: A system of healthcare delivery that aims to provide a generalized structure and focus when managing the use, access, cost, quality, and effectiveness of healthcare services. It links the patient to provider services.

Managed Competition: A state of healthcare delivery in which a large number of consumers choose among health plans that offer similar benefits. In theory, competition is based on cost and quality and limits high prices and improves quality of care.

Maximum Medical Improvement (MMI), Maximum Medical Recovery (MMR): When the injured worker has recovered from injuries to a level that a physician states further treatment will not substantively change the medical outcome. This does not necessarily mean that the injured worker is back to baseline.

Medicaid: A joint federal/state program that provides basic health insurance for persons with disabilities, or who are poor, or who receive certain government income support benefits (such as Social Security Income) and who meet income and resource limitations. Benefits vary by state. Also referred to as "Title XIX" of the Social Security Act of 1966.

Medicaid Waiver: The federal government "waives" certain Medicaid rules so a state may select a portion of its Medicaid population to receive specialized services not otherwise available to such recipients. Waiver programs provide states with flexibility to serve individuals with substantial long-term care needs at home or in the community rather than in an institution. The program was authorized under Section 1915(c) of the Social Security Act.

Medical Durable Power of Attorney: A legal document that names a surrogate decision-maker for a patient in the event that the patient becomes unable to make his or her own healthcare decisions.

Medically Necessary: The supplies and services needed to diagnose and treat a medical condition in accordance with nationally recognized standards.

Medicare: A nationwide, federally administered health insurance program that covers the cost of hospitalization, medical care, and some related services for eligible persons. Medicare is divided into Part A and Part B. Part A covers inpatient hospital costs (currently reimbursed prospectively using the DRG system). Medicare pays for pharmaceuticals provided in hospitals but not for those provided in outpatient settings. Part A is also called the Supplementary Medical Insurance Program. Part B covers outpatient costs for Medicare patients (currently reimbursed retrospectively).

Minimum Data Set (MDS): The assessment tool used in skilled nursing facilities to place patients into Resource Utilization Groups (RUGs), which determine a facility's reimbursement rate.

Monitoring: The ongoing process of gathering information from relevant sources about the activities and/or services of a case management plan. Monitoring enables the case manager to determine the plan's effectiveness.

Negligence: Failure to act as a reasonable person. Behavior is contrary to that of any ordinary person facing similar circumstances.

Network Model HMO: A type of insurance plan that contracts with groups of physicians and other providers in a network of care with organized referral patterns. Networks allow providers to practice outside the HMO.

Neuropsychological Evaluation: A test performed to acquire information regarding the cognitive, behavioral, motor, linguistic, and executive functioning of an individual. This is done after a head injury to determine areas of deficits.

Nonmaleficence: Refraining from doing harm to others; that is, emphasizing quality care outcomes.

Outcome: The results and consequences of a healthcare process. It represents the cumulative effects of one or more processes on a client at a defined point in time. It may be the result of care received or not received. A good outcome is a result that achieved the intended goal.

Outcome and Assessment Information Set (OASIS): A prospective nursing assessment completed by home health agencies when the patient enters home health services. Scoring determines the Home Health Resource Group (HHRG).

Outcome Indicators: Measures of quality and cost of care. Metrics used to examine and evaluate the results of the care delivered.

Outcomes Management: The use of information and knowledge gained from outcomes monitoring to achieve optimal patient outcomes through improved clinical decision-making and service delivery.

Outcomes Measurement: The systematic, quantitative observation, at a point in time, of outcome indicators.

Outcomes Monitoring: The repeated measurement over time of outcome indicators in a manner that permits causal inferences about which patient characteristics, care processes, and resources produced the observed patient outcomes.

Patient Abandonment: Terminating the relationship with the patient without giving reasonable notice or providing a competent replacement, resulting in a lack of necessary medical care.

Payer: The party responsible for reimbursement of healthcare providers and agencies for services rendered, such as the Centers for Medicare and Medicaid Services or managed care organizations.

Peer Review: Review by healthcare practitioners of services ordered or furnished by other practitioners in the same professional field.

Peer Review Organization (PRO): A federal program established by the Tax Equity and Fiscal Responsibility Act of 1982 that monitors the medical necessity and quality of services provided to Medicare and Medicaid beneficiaries under the prospective payment system.

Per Diem: A daily reimbursement rate for all inpatient hospital services provided to one patient, regardless of the actual cost to the healthcare provider. The rate can vary by service (such as medical, surgical, mental health, etc.) or can be uniform regardless of intensity of services.

Performance Improvement: The continuous study and adaptation of the functions and processes of a healthcare organization to increase the probability of achieving desired outcomes and to better meet the needs of patients.

Physical Disability: A bodily defect that interferes with education, development, adjustment, or rehabilitation; generally refers to crippling conditions and chronic health problems but usually does not include single sensory handicaps such as blindness or deafness.

Physician Hospital Organization: An organization of physicians and hospitals responsible for negotiating healthcare contracts with such third-party payers as managed care organizations.

Planning: The process of determining specific objectives, goals, and actions designed to meet the client's needs as identified through the assessment process. The plan should be action-oriented and time-specific.

Point-of-Service (POS) Plan: A type of health plan in which the covered person can elect to receive service from either a participating or a non-participating provider, with different benefit levels associated with each. Members usually pay substantially high premiums, deductibles, and coinsurance.

Practice Guidelines: Systematically developed statements on medical practices that assist a practitioner in making decisions about appropriate diagnostic and therapeutic healthcare services for specific medical conditions. They are usually developed by authoritative professional societies and organizations, such as the American Medical Association.

Preadmission Certification: An element of utilization review that examines the need for proposed services before admission to an institution, to determine the appropriateness of the setting, procedures, treatments, and length of stay.

Preauthorization/Precertification: The process of obtaining and documenting advanced approval from the health plan by the provider before delivering needed medical services. This is required when services are of a nonemergent nature.

Preferred Provider Organization (PPO): An insurance program in which contracts are established with preferred providers of medical care. The benefit contract usually provides the covered individual significantly better benefits for services received from preferred providers, thus encouraging members to use these providers. Covered persons are generally allowed benefits for nonparticipating provider services, usually on an indemnity basis with high copayments.

Primary Care: The point at which the patient first seeks assistance from the medical care system. It also is the care of simpler and more common illnesses.

Primary Care Provider: A healthcare provider who assumes ongoing responsibility for the patient in both health maintenance and treatment. Usually responsible for orchestrating the medical care process either by caring for the patient or by referring the patient for specialized diagnosis and treatment. Primary care providers include general or family practitioners, internists, pediatricians, and sometimes OB/GYN doctors.

Principal Diagnosis: The chief complaint or health condition that required the patient's admission to the hospital for care.

Principal Procedure: A procedure performed for definitive rather than diagnostic treatment. It is necessary for treating a certain condition. It is usually related to the primary diagnosis.

Prospective Payment System: A healthcare payment system used by the federal government since 1983 for reimbursing healthcare providers/agencies for care provided to Medicare and Medicaid participants. The payment is fixed and based on the operating costs of the patient's diagnosis.

Prospective Review: A method of reviewing possible hospitalization before admission to determine necessity and estimated length of stay.

Provider: A person or entity that provides healthcare services. This includes both practitioners and facilities.

Quality Assurance: The use of activities and programs to ensure the quality of patient care. These activities and programs are designed to monitor, prevent, and correct quality deficiencies and noncompliance with the standards of care and practice.

Quality Improvement: An array of techniques and methods used to collect and analyze data gathered in the course of current healthcare practices in a defined care setting. It is used to identify and resolve problems in the system and to improve the processes and outcomes of care.

Quality Indicator: A predetermined measure for assessing quality; a metric.

Quality Management: A formal, planned, systematic, and organization-wide (or network-wide) approach to the monitoring, analysis, and improvement of organization performance. The purpose is to continually improve the extent to which providers conform to defined standards, the quality of patient care and the services provided, and the likelihood of achieving desired patient outcomes.

Quality Monitoring: A process used to ensure that care is being delivered at or above acceptable quality standards as identified by the organization or national guidelines.

Reasonable Accommodation: Making existing facilities used by employees readily accessible and usable by individuals with disabilities. This may include job restructuring, part-time or modified work schedules, acquisition or modification of equipment or devices, and other similar accommodations for individuals with disabilities.

Rehabilitation:

1) Restoration of form and function following an illness or injury.

2) Restoration of an individual's capability to achieve the fullest possible life compatible with his abilities and disabilities.

3) The development of a person to the fullest physical, psychological, social, vocational, avocational, and educational potential consistent with his/her physiological or anatomical impairment and environmental limitations.

Relative Weight: An assigned number intended to reflect the relative resource consumption associated with a Diagnosis Related Group. The higher the relative weight, the greater the payment/reimbursement to the hospital.

Release: The relinquishment of a right, claim, or privilege, by a person in whom it exists or to whom it accrues, to the person against whom it might have been demanded or enforced.

Resource Utilization Group (RUG): Classifies skilled nursing facility patients into 7 major hierarchies and 44 groups. Based on the Minimum Data Set, the patient is classified into the most appropriate group that provides the greatest reimbursement.

Respondeat Superior: A legal term meaning an employer is liable in certain cases for the wrongful acts of his or her employees. Literally, "Let the master respond."

Retrospective Review: A form of medical records review that is conducted after the patient's discharge to track appropriateness of care and consumption of resources.

Risk Management: The science of the identification, evaluation, and treatment of financial (and clinical) loss. A program that attempts to provide positive avoidance of negative results.

Risk Sharing: The process whereby a Health Maintenance Organization and its contracted provider each accept partial responsibility for the financial risk and rewards of caring for the plan members assigned to that specific provider.

Root Cause Analysis: A process used by healthcare providers and administrators to identify the basic or causal factors that contribute to variation in performance and outcomes or that underlie the occurrence of a sentinel event.

Self-Insurer: An employer that meets the state legal and financial requirements to assume all of its healthcare costs for its employees. The employer assumes all risk and pays for the losses. The employer may contract with an insurance carrier or others to provide certain essential services, however.

Severity of Illness: An acuity of illness criteria that identifies the presence of significant/debilitating symptoms, deviations from the patient's normal values, or unstable/abnormal vital signs or laboratory findings.

Short-Term Disability Income Insurance: The provision to pay benefits to a covered disabled person/employee as long as he or she remains disabled, up to a specific period not exceeding two years.

Skilled Care: Patient care services that require delivery by a licensed professional, such as a registered nurse, physical therapist, occupational therapist, speech pathologist, or social worker.

Social Security Disability Income (SSDI): Federal benefit program sponsored by the Social Security Administration. Disability benefits received from a deceased or disabled parent depend upon money contributed to the Social Security program by the individual involved and/or the parent involved.

Staff Model HMO: An HMO model in which physicians are on the staff of the HMO and provide care exclusively for the health plan enrollees. The most rigid HMO model.

Standard (Individual): An authoritative statement by which a profession defines the responsibilities for which its practitioners are accountable.

Standard (Organization): An authoritative statement that defines the performance expectations, structures, or processes that must be substantially in place in an organization to enhance the quality of care.

Standards of Care: Statements that delineate the care expected to be provided to all clients. They include predefined outcomes of care that clients can expect from providers and are accepted within the community of professionals, based upon the best scientific knowledge, current outcomes data, and clinical expertise.

Standards of Practice: Statements of the acceptable level of performance, or expectations for professional intervention or behavior, associated with one's professional practice. They are generally formulated by practitioner organizations based upon clinical expertise and the most current research findings.

Statute: An act of a legislature declaring, commanding, or prohibiting an action, in contrast to unwritten common law.

Subacute Care Facility: A healthcare facility for patients who require a level of care between acute care hospital and conventional skilled nursing facility, in regards to the intensity of services.

Subpoena: A process commanding a witness to appear and give testimony in court.

Supplemental Security Income (SSI): Federal financial benefit program sponsored by the Social Security Administration.

Supported Employment: Paid employment for persons with developmental disabilities who, without long-term support, are unlikely to succeed in a regular job. Supported employment facilitates competitive work in integrated work settings for individuals with the most severe disabilities (e.g., psychiatric, intellectual, or learning disabilities or traumatic brain injury) for whom competitive employment has not traditionally occurred, and who, because of the nature and severity of their disability, need ongoing support in order to perform their job. Supported employment provides assistance such as job coaches, transportation, assistive technology, specialized job training, and individually tailored supervision.

Third Party Administrator (TPA): An organization separate from the insuring organization that handles administrative functions such as utilization review and claims processing. TPAs are used to cost-effectively administer health benefits.

Ticket to Work Program: A voluntary program administered by the Social Security Administration for adults who receive benefits based on disability under the Social Security Disability Insurance (SSDI) program and/or the Supplemental Security Income (SSI) program. The purpose of the program is to provide expanded options for accessing employment services, vocational rehabilitation services, or other support services needed to enter, maintain, and advance in employment.

Tort: A civil wrong for which a private individual may recover money damages, arising from a breach of duty created by law.

Tort Liability: The legal requirement that a person responsible, or at fault, shall pay for the damages and injuries caused.

Total Disability: An illness or injury that prevents an individual from continuously performing any and all duties pertaining to his or her occupation or engaging in any other type of work.

Utilization Management: Review of services to ensure they are medically necessary, provided in the most appropriate care setting, and at or above quality standards.

Utilization Review: A mechanism used by some insurers and employers to evaluate healthcare on the basis of appropriateness, necessity, and quality.

Utilization Review Accreditation Commission (URAC): A not-for-profit organization that provides accreditation for utilization review services offered by freestanding agencies. It is also known as the American Accreditation Health Care Commission.

Veracity: The act of telling the truth.

Vocational Assessment: Identifies the individual's strengths, skills, interests, abilities, and rehabilitation needs. Accomplished through on-site situational assessments at local businesses and in community settings.

Vocational Evaluation: The comprehensive assessment of vocational aptitudes and potential. It uses information about a person's history and medical and psychological status, as well as information from appropriate vocational testing, which may use paper and pencil instruments, work samples, simulated workstations, or assessment in a real work environment.

Vocational Rehabilitation: Cost-effective case management by a skilled professional to facilitate an injured worker's expedient return to suitable gainful employment with a minimal degree of disability. The healthcare professional understands the medical and vocational services necessary for the injured worker to return to work.

Vocational Rehabilitation Counselor: A rehabilitation counselor who specializes in vocational counseling, such as guiding handicapped persons in the selection of a vocation or occupation.

Vocational Testing: The measurement of vocational interests, attitudes, and ability using standardized, professionally accepted psychomotor procedures.

Work Adjustment: The use of real or simulated work activity under close supervision at a rehabilitation facility or other work setting to develop appropriate work behaviors, attitudes, or personal characteristics.

Work Adjustment Training: A program for persons whose disabilities limit them from obtaining competitive employment. It typically includes a system of goal-directed services to improve problem areas such as attendance, work stamina, punctuality, dress, hygiene, and interpersonal relationships with co-workers and supervisors. Services can continue until objectives are met or until there has been noted progress. It may include practical work experience or extended employment.

Work Conditioning: An intensive, work-related, goal-oriented conditioning program. The objective of the program is to restore physical capacity and function to enable the patient/client to return to work. It is designed specifically to restore the following systemic functions:

Neuromusculoskeletal functions, such as joint integrity and mobility, or muscle performance, including strength, power, and endurance

Motor function, such as motor control and motor learning

Range of motion, including muscle length

Cardiovascular/pulmonary functions, such as aerobic capacity/endurance, circulation, and ventilation and respiration/gas exchange

Work Hardening: A highly structured, goal-oriented, and individualized intervention program that provides clients with a transition between the acute injury stage and a safe, productive return to work. Treatment is designed to maximize each individual's ability to return to work safely with less likelihood of repeat injury. Work hardening programs are multidisciplinary in nature and use real or simulated work activities designed to restore physical, behavioral, and vocational functions. They address the issues of productivity, safety, physical tolerances, and worker behaviors.

Work Modification: Altering the work environment to accommodate a person's physical or mental limitations by making changes in equipment, in the methods of completing tasks, or in job duties.

Work Rehabilitation: A structured program of graded physical conditioning/ strengthening exercises and functional tasks in conjunction with real or simulated job activities. Treatment is designed to improve the individual's cardiopulmonary function, neuromusculoskeletal functions (strength, endurance, movement, flexibility, stability, and motor control), biomechanical/human performance levels, and psychosocial aspects as they relate to the demands of work. Work rehabilitation provides a transition between acute care and return to work while addressing the issues of safety, physical tolerances, work behaviors, and functional abilities.

Workers' Compensation: An insurance program that provides medical benefits and replacement of lost wages for persons suffering from injury or illness that occurred in or was caused by the workplace. It is an insurance system for industrial and work injury, regulated primarily by the states, but regulated by the federal government in certain specified occupations.

What's Next?

Congratulations! You have completed an important part of preparing to sit for your CCM Certification. If you have found the information in this book helpful and would like information on additional resources to help you pass the CCM exam, please visit: CaseManagementStudyGuide.com/pass

There you can download your free companion workbook to *CCM Certification Made Easy*. You will also be able to contact me from the contact page. I would love to hear feedback.

ABOUT THE AUTHOR

Deanna Cooper Gillingham, RN, CCM, has been a Registered Nurse since 1994 and a Case Manager since 2011, working both complex and transplant case management. She has worked in a variety of clinical settings, including med surge, dialysis, oncology, hospice, SICU, LDRP, L&D, and GI Lab. She has also worked as a travel nurse, agency nurse, and patient service representative.

She is a contributing author in New York Times Bestselling Author Joel Comm's book, *So What Do You Do? Vol 2* (Morgan James Publishing, 2014). Deanna has a website and blog at CaseManagementStudyGuide.com, where she has helped countless Case Managers pass the CCM exam.